In praise of De
OYR Summ.

"When colleagues ask, 'Why Calgary?', my perennial reply is, 'Because Denise Clarke doesn't live in Toronto.' Absorbing One Yellow Rabbit performances uncorked the bottle for me, and they are why I keep going: the body as ally, literature as flesh, ebullience to woe in the angling of an eyebrow. Staying wild. Denise assembles in these pages all of the elements which, in the 'laboratory inside your own skin' will combine to bubble, froth and spill over in the most delightful and unexpected ways. It is a gift." — *Kris Demeanor, Musician and Poet*

"Clarke invented a highly original theatrical language, a personal expression of gesture and word that seamlessly integrates both dance and storytelling into powerful narrative that resonates deeply with the human spirit and emotionally transports her audiences." — *Heather Elton, Writer, Photographer, Yogini*

"Denise Clarke is known for her tremendous generosity as a dance/theatre artist, and this book extends that generosity to a much broader community. The ripple effect will be extensive."
— *Anne Flynn, Dancer and Educator*

"To be at the Summer Lab in OYR is like upgrading the operating system of my creational computer and resetting my physical capabilities."— *Zaide Silvia Gutiérrez, Actress*

"A brilliant look inside the galaxy of principles that have made the Rabbits' hearts tick. A kind of textbook for beautiful freaks."
— *Karen Hines, Actress, Playwright*

"The Lab is serious work for playful people. It is *the* laboratory for our art form: singular in Canada, unique in our profession, and something to be treasured."
— *Peter Hinton OC, Stage Director, Playwright*

"What is striking to me is that Denise has found a way to be both rigorously disciplined and playfully spontaneous, all at the same time! It might not sound like much but this combination is to me the holy grail for all performing artists and something I know I will be searching for the rest of my life."
— *Jakob Koranyi, Cellist and Educator*

"Wise words from one of Canada's most beloved theatre practitioners." — *Clem Martini, Playwright and Educator*

"Denise Clarke is not only an extraordinary artist, she is also extraordinarily generous. For more than two decades at the Summer Lab Intensive, she has enthusiastically imparted the secrets to One Yellow Rabbit's unique and successful style of performance theatre. Her 'big secret' is an open secret, a big-hearted desire to have others experience the thrill and fulfillment of creation that has sustained her through a remarkable career and is palpable in the pages of this book."
— *Martin Morrow, Author,* Wild Theatre: The History of One Yellow Rabbit

"The words Denise shares with us are rigorous and yet playful. She knows how to tell a story which has a purpose that is both entertaining and mind-changing – life changing."
— *John Murrell OC, Author and Playwright*

"To be in her presence and to share the room with this phenomenally gifted artist and teacher is a truly transformative experience. This insightful, generous, and elegantly practical guide is the next best thing!"
—*David Rhymer, Composer and Musician*

"It's impossible to imagine theatre in Calgary these past several decades without the immense contribution and talent of Denise Clarke. And yet thanks to her tireless work inspiring an entire generation of artists through the OYR Intensive it runs far deeper than can be seen on the surface."
— *Eugene Stickland, Novelist and Playwright*

The
Big
Secret
Book

Photo: Ryan Bartlett

Denise Clarke

The Big Secret Book

An Intense Guide for Creating Performance Theatre

For Katelyn (the unique) Love Denise

UpRoute
Books & Media

An Imprint of
Durvile Publications

UpRoute Books and Media
An Imprint of Durvile Publications Ltd.
Calgary, Alberta, Canada

Copyright © 2018 by Denise Clarke

National Library of Canada
Cataloging in Publications Data
Written by: Clarke, Denise

The Big Secret Book
An Intense Guide for Creating Performance Theatre
Information on this title at durvile.com and uproute.ca
ISBN: 978-1-988824-11-6 (pbk)
ISBN: 978-1-988824-12-3 (ebook)
ISBN: 978-1-988824-25-3 (audiobook)

Book Five in the UpRoute Artist Series

1. Performance 2. Theatre 3. Acting 4. Directing 5. Choreography
First edition | First printing 2018 | Printed in Canada
Book designed by Lorene Shyba

First edition, first printing. 2018
Durvile Publications would like to acknowledge the support of the
Alberta Government through the Alberta Media Fund.

Alberta

All rights reserved. No part of this publication may be produced,
stored in a retrieval system or transmitted in any form or
by any means without prior written consent.
Contact Durvile Publications Ltd. for details.

The statements, views, and opinions contained in this publication
are solely those of the authors.

For the Rabbits,
all of you,
my colleagues,
my inspiration,
my friends.

Also by Denise Clarke

*Featherland: The Magical True Tale
of an Extraordinary Love Triangle*

Contents

Foreword by John Murrell   1
Preface. Who Are You Now?   5

PART ONE   9
The Player

One. Beginning	11
Two. Your Physical Practice	19
Three. Preferences	41
Four. Creating Personal Vocabs and Repetition	53
Five. Precision, Economy and Relaxation	163

PART TWO   79
The Observer, the Observed and the Process of Observation

Six. The Theatre of Perception	81
Seven. *Punctum* and *Studium*	93
Eight. Silence, Exile, and Cunning	103
Nine. The Burroughs Effect and Cut-Ups	109

PART THREE 9
Setting Up the Room and Making a Performance Plan

Ten. Who Does What	125
Eleven. Creating the Performance Plan	137
Twelve. Concept Development	147
Thirteen. Harnessing the Power of Limitations	157
Fourteen. Material Survey and Arrangement	171
Fifteen. Final Presentation	183
Conclusion	188

Acknowledgments 191
Index 192
About the Author 198

Foreword

JOHN MURRELL

THE BIG SECRET BOOK is a generous book. It offers us so much, including:
- A down-to-earth guide to becoming a healthy, practicing creator of theatre;
- An honest and entertaining glimpse into the history of the unique One Yellow Rabbit Performance Theatre, and into the equally unique Summer Lab Intensive which Denise Clarke invented along with her gifted OYR colleagues and others;
- Clear signposts to help theatre-makers know when they are going too fast or too slow ('bigger it up or smaller it down'); when they are being good companions within a creative group and when they are reducing their own creativity and the creativity of others (too much or too little generosity with their own immediate opinions).

And so much more.

Having worked with and observed Denise for many years now, I understand that her 'Personal Sidebars' in this book are as candid as she is herself. These are examples of her own creative challenges and creative solutions, testaments to how she never assumes but rather searches, how willing she is to make creative 'mistakes' which lead to creative discoveries. She has devoted her life to this. We can all benefit from her candor.

My own experience with One Yellow Rabbit goes back to the days when I was the company's 'officer' as Head of the Theatre Section of The Canada Council For The Arts. My fellow officers at the Council were sometimes uncertain about how to evaluate or appreciate OYR's creative impulses and achievements. I was somewhat uncertain too, at first – but that didn't stop me. From the start, I wanted to understand the vision and the methods of these artists, from the inside out, as well as from the outside in. This eventually led me, soon after I left the Canada Council, to propose creating a piece of theatre for and with the Rabbits. That was in the early nineties, and since that time I've been part of three other theatrical enterprises which benefitted from the company's intensity with regard to both how performance is created, and how it is presented to its ultimate destination, the audience.

In between two of these interactive creative explorations with the Rabbits, I was asked by Denise to be part of the original group of mentors/animators of her inaugural Summer Lab Intensive in 1997. I hesitated for a couple of weeks to accept Denise's invitation, only because I was unsure what I had to bring to the inspirational table alongside such accomplished chefs as Blake Brooker, Ronnie Burkett, Chris Cran, and Denise herself. Upon further reflection, I realized I was merely being a coward. Denise would not have asked me to be part of the team unless she knew I could 'play'. During the years when I was a daily part of the Lab, I found out a lot more about how serious play, in tandem with a solid artistic practice, is the essence of generating theatrical performance.

Denise has organized her book like the consummate author she is, having written and contributed to the writing of a number of playscripts which are both playable and profound. But she writes about performance as only a consummate performer can. She describes setbacks as ultimate victories. She describes victories as signposts along the path to perfecting the organism, while alerting us to the fact that perfection is not a thing which we achieve, but rather a thing to which we forever aspire.

I consider myself fortunate in having had frequent and lengthy – sometimes five- and six-hour – conversations with Denise about the art, the practice, the pain, the joy. To read this book is like being in on those conversations. The words she shares with us are rigorous and yet playful. She knows how to tell a story which has a purpose that is both entertaining and mind-changing, life-changing.

Enjoy this book the way Denise enjoys creating theatre, seriously, playfully, intensely, with time allotted to your own thoughts, your own struggles – then returning to the book, to the world in which Denise has lived and continues to live: a world of outward and inward journeys – journeys in search of gifts which can be shared through that most exhilarating of festivities, the theatre.

This is a generous book, offered to us at a very ungenerous time in human history. Make use of it whenever you need, whenever you can. — *John Murrell, O.C.*

Photo: Heather Elton

Preface

Who Are You Now?

It is a simple question that raises a complex answer.

This is about you. You are a writer, an actor, a director, a dancer, a choreographer, a composer, or a designer. You are one of these, some of these, or all of these. Your unique and highly individual self has come into the world and somehow you have decided on theatre or theatre has decided on you. There is a drive to express and to communicate your truth in community with fellow artists and, very importantly, with the observers, the witnesses, the audience.

It makes no matter whether you want the observers to laugh, to cry, to think, to tap their toes, to understand, or to make change, you will invite them to come to a place, a seeing and listening place, to observe you, sometimes alone but usually with others as you strive to achieve your desired effect. You must investigate your **personal aesthetic** and harness your skills in order to find your own voice. Even to begin can be daunting. Is there a secret to making it all work? Are there a thousand secrets? What if it doesn't work? You could fail at your goal and so should you stop at once and never try again?

Most likely there is someone in your head, a teacher, a family member, another artist who you fear will not approve. They sit silently in your consciousness, judging you and although you can sometimes overcome their judgment and rejoice in creation, they more often overwhelm your efforts. What is the secret to silencing them and ridding yourself of that crippling voice? Unless they are in the room beside you, impeding your progress, (in which case you should perhaps quit doing that and stop working with them), then here is one of the greatest secrets of all theatre making: you are the creator and this is your creation but you are giving all the power to an imagined judge! Flip that switch. You are the judge stopping you, so **Stop Judging**. That voice will lose power and eventually you can politely ignore it. Ban it. Ask it to leave. The beginning is not the time to judge and now you, my friend, can get to work.

Build yourself a laboratory inside your own skin so you can start the investigation of your **personal aesthetic**. Having done so as both a soloist and with the glorious camaraderie of the One Yellow Rabbit (OYR) Performance Ensemble, and as the Director of the OYR Summer Lab Intensive, I have been engaged in longtime active research inside my own skin-lab.

One Yellow Rabbit's Big Secret Theatre is a place where everyone's voice is always welcome within the boundaries of good **etiquette and generosity**; holding the floor for too long is not really on, but reflection, humour and riffing, and specific emotional or intellectual response, is. Excellence and fun were mixed into the origins and commitment to making work that played up to a 'talented' audience.

Although we've always seen ourselves as more of a rock band than a theatre company, we observe a somewhat traditional hierarchy when we gather as the OYR Ensemble. For most of our time together that meant Blake Brooker in the director's chair, myself staging the work and performing, the late Richard McDowell as the composer, or as he called himself, the 'compuser' and the late Michael Green, along with Andy Curtis, and a rotation of other honoured guest artists making up the rest of the performing company. We can never replace our brothers who left their bodies but we continue to this day working and playing with our extended ensemble of collaborators.

Much of the working vocabulary that we share has developed over thirty-five years. You will read them throughout as **Bolded Text** and they may inform you as to how the working vocabulary has served us. To credit each and every notion to one of us would be exhausting, however it behooves me to name Blake Brooker Artistic Director of OYR who, early on, defined many of the early ideas that became our values, techniques and beliefs and spurred us to action.

Inspired by meeting colleagues wherever we toured who had 'how and why' questions about our work, I designed the OYR Summer Lab Intensive in 1997 to investigate and play in search of some answers. The first few years, my colleagues, Blake Brooker, playwright John Murrell, marionette master Ronnie Burkett, and visual artist Chris Cran joined me as we embarked on a mission to further develop a working vocabulary that we could share with the participants and at this writing, that vocabulary has continued to grow and serve Blake, Chris, and me as the Lab faculty.

Sometimes there are obstacles to creation and many fine artists have made their way to the OYR Lab to do their own active research and investigate those obstacles within our prepared three weeks of guided instruction. This is a book that may encourage and inspire you to build your own lab inside your own skin and to carry that lab within you no matter what your preferred discipline or how many others you choose to work with. Let's use the language of the OYR Lab. Stretch it, change it, let it morph into anything that makes sense to you, because this is about you but … get to work!   — *Denise Clarke*

Part One

The Player

Photo: David Cooper

Chapter One

BEGINNING

Be patient toward all that is unsolved in your heart and try to love the questions themselves, like locked rooms and like books that are now written in a very foreign tongue. Do not now seek the answers, which cannot be given you because you would not be able to live them. And the point is, to live everything. Live the questions now. Perhaps you will then gradually, without noticing it, live along some distant day into the answer.

— Rainer Maria Rilke

Hold Your Questions

Sometimes questions are drowned by premature answers. People are **meaning-making machines** drawn inexorably to making meaning of anything that perplexes them and invites inquiry. If a question arises, we are compelled to find the answer quickly as though it is the imperative to continuing. And of course there are times when that is the case. But what if we imagine the questions as small engines for the imagination, steeping in us, growing more exact and articulate, inspiring the intuitive self to expand and delight in the mystery. Often artists are driven by the urge to create but the exact nature of that creation is vague and unformed.

The simple act of allowing oneself to **embrace the questions** internally and then make preparations for the answers to reveal themselves, could be one of the definitions of creative practice. Maybe the given is that there is an unending river of questions moving us through our aesthetic likes and dislikes, and the impulse to meet each question with a definitive answer could be as stultifying as the feeling of not knowing. Perhaps it is just as well to gather and arrange some intuitively chosen elements around you, maybe it's a book or a piece of music, a garment or just several ideas; something is inspiring you. Gather and arrange those inspirational elements around yourself and begin actions that will engage the imagination and lead into the work. The answers will reveal themselves in playable solutions and theatrical inventions.

Permission

To prepare for making art invites a million excuses to do something else. It can be difficult to motivate oneself. In the theatre, we are so often dependent on the relationships we have to others. "I am not a real actor if I don't get the gig after an audition." Or, "if my play is not produced." Or, … fill in the blank with your own discipline. This may indeed be the case if you are dealing exclusively with your career path. Obviously there are real concerns about keeping oneself alive and out from under the wheel of crushing poverty and questions of self worth. But for our purposes here, let's put that aside and deal first of all with the impulse to create which may have led you to read this. Can one be an artist if one is not employed and paid as an artist? Let's argue that yes, one can. First and foremost, art is a calling from what we might refer to as the soul. From inside a person. It's a longing or an inchoate feeling. A desire to shape internalized sensations into something that might be shareable with the world. One could say that it has to do with spirit or the divine in us. We find ourselves devoted

The Lab: The practice of being still and breathing provides an opportunity to go deeper into complicated desires.

to a particular idea which might soothe that inchoate longing, eventually giving it form that could also soothe those we invite to watch us. We have to locate it, struggle with it, wrestle it, name it and define it, then coax it from ourselves in order to begin that shaping process. But how? It could be that too often the question of 'how' halts the investigation and the mysteries pile up so that the artist feels a sense of failure even before beginning.

Imagine instead that the 'how' question is the engine and it has a vehicle to propel. All too often, an artist is halted before they begin by searching the universe inside themselves and the outside world for **permission**. It may sound reductive to suggest that it's a simple question of permission but most creators who don't have a track record, and even some who do, are shy and slightly disbelieving that they might throw their hats into the creative ring. That voice of judgment is there saying, "You? Really? You want to make a hit show? Write a smash play? Choreograph something gorgeous? Devise a fabulous new piece of performance from scratch?" The key here is that so often we have put the cart before the horse. We already want success in our game plan. We want to do something that in the end is excellent.

Well, of course we do, but that is not our business at the beginning of our work. Discernment and the judging of which ideas will make the final cut most certainly do come later but if we start there, chances are slim for the intuitive authentic voice to emerge. So let's say that this reading gives you permission to begin. The stern **judge** has been invited out of the scene. The inchoate desire, the song that needs to be sung, the dance calling you, the comedy tickling your belly, the idea that won't let go has been given **permission** to begin its journey outwards.

If we are to have a snowball's chance in hell of 'success' and excellence then we might be wise to begin with a practice that will prepare us most effectively to make something that is true and authentic and finds its audience.

Now you need to design your **practice**.

Your Practice

Inspiration exists in the language used by both visual artists and yogis/yoginis. Both refer to what they do as "my practice." It's lovely because it is personal and has such ownership and strength.

> This activity that I love, that I desire to engage in is something I can call mine. It's my practice. I want to practice my art. I want to repeat things so that I will be

deeply familiar with that which I love and desire. I don't go into my studio to paint a 'great painting', I go in to paint because I love painting. I love colour, form, composition and content, so much that I am willing to repeat the act as much as I can. And from that activity I will later discern which paintings are great. Regardless, it is my practice.

Yoginis/yogis also call what they do "my practice." It might sound precious but it is precious. All you need is a mat and the space to lay it down. Whatever happens from that point on is deeply personal and introduces the practitioner to themselves and their process of investigation over and over. They say yoga teaches yoga which could mean that to commit to just laying the mat on the floor and yourself on the mat is an opportunity to go deeper into this process of investigating you and your complicated desires.

Your practice will deepen and will serve you as you continue mining for gold in your chosen field of devotion. It would be necessary here to posit that the goal is to live your practice in as healthful a manner as possible. History can serve up many examples of artists who suffered terribly for their art, but it is the 21st century and this book is dedicated to the ambition of art making that gives the artist succor and some joy and enhances their lives. Perhaps that is a utopic notion but it could be that by accessing your creative potential, you will also be a better citizen and aid in making our society a better one to share.

With Michael Green

DOING LEONARD COHEN

"Connect nothing: F. shouted. Place things side by side on your arborite table, if you must but connect nothing!"
— Leonard Cohen

IN 1997, One Yellow Rabbit received permission from Leonard Cohen to make the show *Doing Leonard Cohen*. Cohen's large body of written work is rich and full of wisdom, humour, and searing honesty and it was overwhelming to imagine how to start, so we gathered all his books and tasked ourselves with reading them out loud to one another, each of us creating a long list of favourite poems and passages of the novel. Once we had read everything, a host of new questions began.

Our decision was to stage a two-act piece with Act 1 featuring a selection of poems and Act 2, an adaptation of Cohen's sexually frenzied amphetamine driven novel, *Beautiful Losers* which is the gloriously dirty, funny love story of the queer F., the Narrator and their passionate relationships to both the Narrator's wife Edith and the Indigenous saint Catherine Tekakwitha.

But how to narrow our long lists of hundreds of poems into a short list? How to adapt the novel? How to stage it? How to connect it all into a coherent presentation? It could have become completely overwhelming if we hadn't seized onto F.'s admonition to the Narrator:

"Connect nothing: F. shouted. **Place things side by side on your arborite table**, if you must but connect nothing!"

The early days of the process were too soon for questions about seamless and constant connection of the sublime poetics and humour of Cohen's work. It would have stymied us, effectively stopping the active work and so instead we embraced the questions and took instruction from the master. We 'placed things side by side on our arborite table' which in our case meant the wall and sticky notes with poem titles in one colour, ideas in another, and physical vocabularies in one more. We decided to hold off on making all the connections and to concentrate instead on individual elements.

And so right from the start, with the long list list of poetic elements narrowing, and the adaptation of the novel underway, we had begun to **seriously play**. Every day we assembled more physical choreographic elements, a walking series of solos, duets, trios and quartets that allowed the viewer to witness snapshots of romantic love, loss, ego and desire. Intentions could turn on a dime, the four actors coupling, loving and flirting or hurting one another with passion or insouciance, anger or tenderness. We were busy and active, committed to learning and retaining a complicated yet intuitive dance that demanded **precision, economy, and relaxation,** while searching for the logical order of the poems. Answers and connections began to make themselves apparent and the layering in and sequencing of text was made easier by everyone's familiarization with all of the elements that we had surrounded ourselves with. The piece was light and full of Cohen's mischief, dark notes, painful truths and beauty and we felt we had served both him and our own aesthetic needs while adding an important piece to our **body of work**.

Chapter Two

YOUR PHYSICAL PRACTICE

Whether or not you are an artist who is drawn to performing physical theatre of any kind, or a committed 'ass in chair' writer, or a director who has no intention of strutting the boards, you have a body and this section will presume to offer instruction on how that body might best be analyzed, optimized, and utilized in your practice. A further presumption will be that to begin the practice/working session with attention to the body is the given. Naturally, each individual or groups will have their own order of attacking their work, and designing their practice. Sometimes there is nothing for it but to leap into an inspired moment and let the muse rip. This might serve instead for those days, weeks, and months when the muse is away and inspiration is unavailable because let's face it, inspiration is a fickle partner and may or may not be there for you but your practice always will.

The yoga mat is a tool that can signal the starting point of your practice. You may decide that you loathe yoga mats and so be it. Whatever your jam, find a room to begin in. Lay down a mat on the floor and step onto it or forget the mat and just find the room. If it is not possible to stand, sit in your wheelchair or any other chair. Everything is adaptable for every artist, beautiful chair practices can be devised with equal detail and effect, it doesn't matter how able-bodied you are, this has application for all physical abilities; but let us begin with your body and the idea of training your nervous system. Bring attention to how you breathe and how you feel.

The Palette of Stillness

Begin from the **palette of stillness**. Stillness is another secret weapon. It is the conscious absence of movement and it signals your nervous system to calm you.

It is well noted that the ability to find stillness onstage will heighten whatever text, movement, and activity surrounds it. All good actors aspire to finding that grounded, still point that will let them deliver a monologue or a moment without distraction. Much goes on in the actor's body and mind when they are approaching that moment and to have the ability to find calm, authentic stillness takes practice and skill. Unconscious flapping hands and nodding heads or shuffling feet can detract from a performance unless that is a character-driven choice.

Too often the player is unaware of this unconscious fidgeting, and an exhortation to 'stay still' by the director can be unnerving. More useful is to explore what it means to come and go from this **palette of stillness**, making all other movement choices more unpredictable so as to engage the viewer and surprise, inform, and delight them with your precise, economical, and relaxed performance.

The control is empowering and lends **authority** to your presence on the stage, which in turn puts the viewer at ease. One can then explode into a riot of thrilling activity or draw the eye to the smallest specific detail, balancing the work along a spectrum from stillness to chaos, which introduces welcome shifts of dynamic intensity. The artist who has that control is more available to serve the work.

Photo: Sean Dennie

SIGN LANGUAGE

IN my solo piece, *Sign Language*, which begins with a comedic ten-minute monologue of modern pretension and neurosis leading into a one-hour non-verbal movement piece, the character finds herself ultimately desirous of spinning out of her neurotic self and into her higher self. Luckily, spinning is something I enjoy and can do on the spot for a strangely long time, in this case six minutes.

While the music soars and I spin in the spotlight, my full-length rippling gold satin skirt creates a liquid-like impression and the long strangeness grows mesmerizing for the viewer. In my palms are small oval mirrors that catch and throw the light. As the soprano's voice reaches its zenith, I stop suddenly and silence fills the air. At the same second that I stop and stand perfectly still, the small mirrors in my palms reflect the overhead light, casting it onto the audience. Without any other movement other than a very subtle tilting of my palms, I actually light the audience with two tiny searchlights, slowly sweeping the rows and sliding over their faces.

The effect is strong. It provides the ending I want; to cease dervish-like yearning and acknowledge those who have been my witnesses for the previous seventy minutes with whom I have shared my illumination. The effect would not have been possible without the surprise of sudden stillness, which long years of practice afforded me.

Relaxation and Training the Nervous System

Whether we enjoy the buzz and heightened thrills of rocking it with our creative colleagues, or prefer pushing ourselves alone in a room with our ideas and a pen, stress and anxieties can surface. For some artists the techniques for and the body memory of relaxation are not only helpful, they are a secret super power. Stress is occasionally a great motivator but most often it gets in the way of intuitive discoveries and unclouded perception.

As you practice stillness and breath control, you will notice your heart rate, how the blood pulses through you, where you feel tightness, how your mood is, and so on. The longer you breathe in stillness, the more the nervous system will calm down so that the process of releasing stress and relaxed self discovery can begin.

The nervous system controls both our voluntary and involuntary responses: voluntary conscious response by the muscles to move as we wish to move, and involuntary responses like breathing, sweating, and digesting our food.

It is possible and desirable to train the nervous system for one essential reason – to combat stress, which creates the stress hormone called cortisol.

We all need a little cortisol to aid us in fight or flight situations like that fabled sabre-toothed tiger on the taiga, but once we are safe, the relaxation response kicks in and allows us to release that cortisol. If we don't make the time/space to allow that to happen before the next stressful event occurs, cortisol builds up and causes chronic stress and anxiety and a host of other side effects. Our cognitive abilities and digestive health become impaired, our blood pressure goes up and the list goes on. It gets tricky to figure out who you are and access your aesthetics and intuition that shape your art-making. Again this applies to all forms of creativity. You might be trying to get that poem to take shape, craft a toast for your best friend's wedding, or you may be preparing to walk into a room full of people waiting for you to direct them. Breathing and inviting calm cannot hurt. Apply this notion to all creative forms: when the body calms, the mind calms, the vocal chords relax and most essentially we enhance the cognitive process towards problem solving. We are better able to focus, remember, evaluate or invent, and whether we make music or dances, write novels or plays, direct others or devise our own work, beginning with stillness and training the nervous system to relax provides an advantage. (See *Tigress at the City Gates* Sidebar on pages 34-35.)

Structural Alignment vs Postural Alignment

Now you're calm. It's a good time to do a postural scan. This is practical and applicable to your wellbeing in general, but in other ways too, like designing a character's posture or analyzing what you're observing in others. Not to put a value judgment on what is 'good posture', but when things are lined up, it is easier and more efficient for the body to move. Also, injuries are less prone to happen if the skeleton is in its most aligned place.

A good example is the image of the jazz musician who plays an upright bass. Their head is thrust out and over the instrument year after year, and one day a neck injury and headaches appear. The player needs to counteract the forward-thrust head with stretching and optimum alignment when not playing and, if possible, during, or the injuries and headaches could affect the ability to play at all. It isn't to say the bass player's posture is 'bad' but it isn't helping them to continue making art.

Posture is deeply personal and an individual's sense of self can be damaged if told that they have 'bad posture'. It is much more important to gauge posture in terms of how it is affecting performance and to frame the investigation in terms of **Structural vs Postural Alignment.**

Structural Alignment is the optimum alignment of the human skeleton in the standing position: head balanced easily over shoulders and rib cage in line with the pelvis on top of the legs following straight down from the hip socket and standing on parallel feet. Picture a marionette standing beneath the puppeteer's control. The marionette can be slumped into an exhausted weak posture by lowering the control slightly or lifted back to its full or truest height, which gives the puppeteer the most control and the marionette the most exquisite expression.

Postural Alignment is what we do to our skeleton by habit and unconscious or conscious placement. You may or may not know that you stand on feet that roll in (pronation) or roll out (supination). Check your shoes to see how the heels wear for a clue. Regardless, that placement of your feet upon the earth will affect the alignment of your knees, pelvis, ribcage, shoulders and head so it's helpful to know your **postural preference**.

A ballet dancer may walk with their feet in outward rotation all the time as a result of the classical form they practice and perform. Especially when exhausted, their body will fall into that famous Chaplinesque placement. It can be a badge of honour to move in this very distinctive way, which marks them as one of the physically elite athletes that ballet dancers are. But it is not an optimal or neutral alignment and, over time, will overstretch ligaments and tendons resulting in weakened knees, or hip or back problems leading to the kind of repetitive stress injury that could take the dancer/player out of action for some time. That sort of 'time out' is tough on anyone's well being.

Then too, consider how it may be a detriment to working in another field. If the ballet dancer wants to transition

PHYSICAL PRACTICE 25

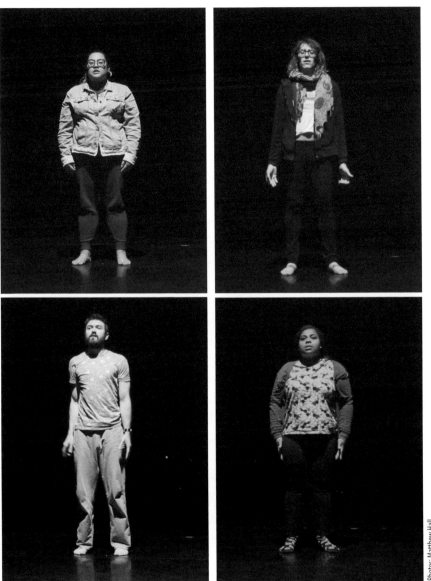

The Lab: Four Labbits, Bianca Miranda, Elise Pallagi, Jeff Charlton, and Keshia Cheesman examining structural vs postural alignment.

into modern dance or become an actor, this highly identifiable posture could be tricky to rid oneself of without stopping to analyze everything that goes into its making. The years of training, the joys and challenges of the career, the ballet dancer's identity is at stake, and it is therefore essential to scan the body and to define the **structural vs postural alignment** without judgment. With knowledge of how they place their feet on the earth and stand or walk in the world, the artist can better optimize their instrument, keeping it in good working order and inviting diverse and exciting challenges for a longer time.

For any individual who has been a long time 'outward rotator', parallel can feel awful and constraining. Trying to slowly turn in and balance posture takes time and conscious effort. You don't 'have' to change it but if you 'want' to change it you might broaden your field of advantage because it also has direct and immediate application to the stage. It registers on the viewer if a player is standing and walking with their feet in outward rotation. It is a distinctive placement, so aesthetically speaking, it would be useful to have the knowledge and the ability to shift between your **postural preference** and a more neutral stance. Otherwise, you run the risk of giving all your work this same appearance.

Simply put, there is greater **movement authority**, efficiency and **precision** if the player can assume the neutral aligned posture and move from it at will. Imagine watching Hamlet's famous speech that begins, "To be or not to be." If the Hamlet in front of you is pacing about like Chaplin, they run the risk of bringing unintentional humour to the speech and it will lack the power it could have if the Prince was aware of posture and gait.

The differently abled artist is able to analyze their posture and define optimal structural alignment in the chair

PHYSICAL PRACTICE 27

The Lab: Neil Cadger in the performance piece "Back to Bite You."
The inherent drama of exploring the kinesphere.

and/or with the crutches in the same manner. The chair-bound writer or director can look at how staying in that chair has affected them and perhaps find balancing activity. If you are plagued by pain related to **postural preferences** like turned-in feet, forward-thrust head, or swayed back and the like, you will benefit from analyzing how you sit, stand, and move. 'Who you are now' is 'how you have lived' and your posture analysis is a tool to aid in self-awareness. (See *Fat Jack Falstaff's Last Hour* Sidebar on pages 36-37.)

Exploring the Kinesphere
Kinesphere is a term borrowed from Laban Movement Analysis (LMA). Developed by Rudolf Laban (1879–1958), and further developed by Irmgard Bartenieff (1900–1981), the study of LMA and/or Bartenieff Fundamentals is a journey into their glorious genius and how they observed,

described, interpreted and documented human movement. It is a field all its own and has contributed immeasurably to the work of thousands of theatre and dance educators and practitioners for much of the 20th century and onwards.

Other influencing giants in the field of movement analysis and efficiency include Frederick Matthias Alexander (1869–1955) inventor of Alexander Technique, Moshé Feldenkrais (1904–1984) inventor of The Feldenkrais Method and Lulu Zweigard (1895–1974) who coined the term, Ideokinesis (imagining movement) and wrote the beautiful book *Human Movement Potential*. To delve into any of these artist visionaries will take you deeper and deeper into the ideas of somatic research and discovery, guaranteed to resonate with curious artists in any field.

The **kinesphere** may best be described as the spherical space you occupy and can explore while you remain rooted to one spot. You can move in silence listening to your breath or score this with any playlist you like that might inspire and encourage you, but start by leaving the feet in as close to parallel position as possible.

Self awareness of your body in space is the goal, but as you move, you will also warm and open yourself to discovering all manner of feelings and sensations: physical and emotional **preferences**, delights, tight places and weaknesses – all of which will occur to you as you move.

The human being in movement is rich with **inherent drama**. A person can be in a neutral posture and by merely collapsing their sternum down, an observer will realize that something is happening to that person. It is always engaging to watch one or many people move from exquisite stillness; their eyes slowly travelling down as the head follows the sternum, sinking deeper and deeper into themselves.

It's as though a narrative begins, some poem of being alive that speaks to the human experience. The narrative suggests humility, grief, loss, perhaps weakness and exhaustion. The observer is engaged because it is recognizable to them, this slump into a soft refusal of verticality. The mover has captured some authority to hold attention by this most simple of motions. Once they reach the end of the downward trajectory and begin to re-ascend, following the line back up to neutral and onwards, lifting the sternum towards the celestial line, the narrative shifts into images of strength, hope, dignity, spiritual yearning, celebration; you will have your own stories flowing through you as you move up and down.

Activity PLAY

You have gone from stillness and simple breathing into scanning your skeleton.

Feel the power of slowly collapsing your sternum down towards your feet allowing your head to follow down the vertical line and back up. Bend your knees and fold yourself in half. After a bit, lift your arms and the story deepens as you gather space into your body or sweep them up your chest and send it out to the far reaches of your **kinesphere**. *Reach behind yourself. Push the hands down beside you. Your feet have not moved away from the rooted spot but much is happening as you respond to each new impulse, as you explore your* **kinesphere** *slowly and with intention. No matter what the action, your engaged, thoughtful exploration takes you into your humanity. And the bonus is that as the nervous system is responding you are also waking up the body/mind connections and the muscles and fascia that hold up your skeleton are warming and lengthening.*

Take the blade of your hand and, bending your knees,

slice down from your hipbones along the imagined crease of your trousers and down the shins to your feet, tracing and tracking the knees. If they knock and fall inwards then play a game of researching how to keep them from doing so. Are your feet parallel or turned out? How wide are they? (Hint: if you want your knees to track down in a straight line with your hips and your middle toes, then your ass will have to stick way out behind you!)

It is also interesting to note that thanks to the simplicity of the movement and to your feet being rooted in the **neutral** position, you have 'placed' yourself and are moving in and out of the optimum **structural alignment** which suggests a kind of noble consciousness. It is very compelling to observe this **inherently dramatic** activity and the viewer also experiences suggested narratives. All kinds of variables influence your movement and your narratives, silence vs. music, what kind of music, the speed with which you move, but regardless, your mood, your circumstances, and your general emotional ambience will be made obvious to you.

You have moved slowly up and down the vertical line into lateral space and through the **kinesphere** with your feet placed as close to parallel as you can.

Now the feet begin to move as you make your own dance, measure your limbs in space and continue to enjoy your music or the silence. Remind yourself of Charlie Chaplin's stance and gait. Look at your own feet and **play**, dancing back and forth between parallel and **outward rotation**.

Feel the core of your body, initiating the movement from your belly, shrinking and stretching the **kinesphere**. This is what Laban called **Shape Flow**.

Initiate with shoulders, hips, go up and down, or reach with your hands into space spiralling into the back. At the *fullest extent of your range of motion if you do not stop the movement, it will curve and follow the sphere in a curvilinear path. This is what Laban called* **Carving**, *a perfect word to describe the nature of the movement someone is doing as they carve through space without stopping.*

Turn your attention to the math of your structure. Explore the various planes that bisect your **kinesphere** *and a different kind of movement emerges, and with it, different narratives. It will look as though you are measuring out where you are or what is beyond you. It goes beyond the internalized* **personal space** *into a more* **public space**. *Draw one hand along the length of the other arm and across your chest, unfolding it until you feel your full wingspan. Exult in your full range of motion, compare it to the narrative that a partial range suggests. Poke your limbs into that space like a five-year-old demonstrating how big they are or as though you are Leonardo's Man. This is what Laban called* **Directional** *movement.*

It's a personal research/dance about who you are and how you move. Once you are dancing and moving your feet, a thousand more physical choices are available to you. Stay slow and conscious or bust out and shake and shimmer without thought. Strike a pose on the beat or stay thoughtful and squat down slowly into your version of Rodin's Thinker. Play and let the narratives unravel. Whatever your soundtrack, play around with levels, balance, repetition, range of movement, and every now and then check in on whether or not you are parallel. Build your dance inside and outside of the kinesphere. Imagine you can step outside yourself and back in. Stretch into other sculptural forms and hold to feel the inherent suggested drama or comedy.

RECAP Design Your Practice

1. Stop Judgment
2. Give Permission
3. Be Still
4. Breathe
5. Scan and Define Your Structural vs your Postural Alignment
6. Understand Parallel
7. Move Vertically then Laterally
8. Explore Kinesphere
9. Play

This chapter has served as a guide to beginning the Physical Practice that the One Yellow Rabbit Lab Intensive begins with each day. The **seriously playful** dance/warm-up/moving meditation, call it what you will, can easily lead into any yoga or tai chi, or a dance of abandon throughout the space. You might want to pump some weights, skip, or lay down and have a little nap at this point. This only serves as a beginning, a reminder to wake up body-mind connection, to breathe, release stress, address postural questions and wellbeing, all of which have served the artists of One Yellow Rabbit (OYR) for thirty-five years.

The Lab: In the mode of pedagogy.

Photos: Matthew Hall

TIGRESS AT THE CITY GATES

IN 1996, I performed the role of the dancer and spy Mata Hari in David Rhymer and Blake Brooker's musical theatre piece, *Tigress At The City Gates*. It was a demanding role, vocally, physically, but especially emotionally. The Dutch-born Margaretha Zelle billed herself as an exotic Hindu temple dancer at the beginning of the 20th century when Orientalism was the fad in Europe. She enjoyed a brief window as a wildly popular star of the salon scene in Paris and beyond. As Mata Hari, her almost nude performances of *Salome's Dance of the Seven Veils* were a sensation for a few short years after which, to support herself, she became a courtesan.

With the First World War approaching, Mata Hari foolishly swirled over borders accepting money for sex from German and French military and government officials who were her preferred lovers.

In 1916, at the age of forty, she met and fell in love with a young soldier who was blinded at the front and to support him she accepted an assignment from French intelligence to utilize the contacts she had made as a courtesan and work as a spy. With military losses mounting, France was searching for scapegoats to blame and in 1917 a German attaché named her in a communiqué seized by French officials. She was arrested, falsely accused of being a double agent and thrown into the horrifying Prison Saint-Lazare, the setting for the OYR show. Flashbacks to her fabulous early days are intercut with the interrogation scenes, which paint her into a corner of increasing danger until she is found guilty and executed by firing squad. The scenes mounted in tension with Michael Green and Andy Curtis, in character, finally screaming at me to admit my guilt, which I refused to do. I had enormous investment in the story and, as in her life she must have done, I felt the horror and fear as my interrogators relentlessly twisted the facts that led to her death. We staged the final scene in front of the rifles as an exquisitely sad and contained song about her loneliness and it was essential that it be played with both dignity and pathos ending on a single piano note and a blackout.

As the weeks of the run went on I fell into a kind of depression and one night, got lost in a monologue which terrified me and stage fright set in. My emotions were more and more difficult to pace and I was stuck in the tragedy of her ending, finding it hard not to play from the beginning as I struggled with the lightness of the youthful scenes.

Finally my fellow player, Elizabeth Stepkowski, took me aside and reminded me that I was being screamed at and then killed every night and suggested that I was holding that stress in my body probably because the last song needed such complete control. I was startled to realize that she was right and that I hadn't found a way to release the stressful daily assault of pain and fear.

I began to take the first few minutes after the show to lock the bathroom door and have a good cry, followed by long calming breaths. I warmed up more carefully and paid attention throughout the first part of my performance, to where I could relax and breathe even while playing towards the sorrowful finalé. Almost immediately the off-stage depression lifted and my stage fright disappeared. I was thrilled to discover that I could actively attend to the built up stress by remembering my techniques for breath control and relaxation. It was a very dramatic lesson to me in balancing my character's journey with my own needs and wellbeing, thereby serving both and the work to best effect.

With John Murrell

FAT JACK FALSTAFF'S LAST HOUR

"Clarke gives her Nell an ample bouncing bosom and a just as ample bouncing buttocks and her performance is every bit as outrageous as her accoutrements."
— *Louis Hobson, The Calgary Herald*

IN 2016, our cherished colleague, playwright John Murrell, wrote the play *Fat Jack Falstaff's Last Hour* and joined the OYR Ensemble to perform it. As Shakespeare's old fool had received only a brief eulogy in *Henry V*, John wrote him a wonderfully funny and moving death scene that, as the title suggests, lasts one full hour. I played Mistress Nell Quickly to John's Falstaff, Andy Curtis was my husband, Ancient Pistol, and Blake Brooker directed us on our set of a ridiculously gigantic bed, which the dying knight is confined to.

The play is most definitely costumed and set in Henry V's early 15th century and I longed to play Nell disguised as much as possible from my normal appearance. Being somewhat lean and small breasted, I decided that by contrast, Nell was a very full-bodied gal with ample bottom and bosom and a saucy sense of herself as an object of desire. Right away my posture was affected and I delighted in the discoveries, making much of her full breasts, a source of great pride to Nell, and feeling my derrière sway behind me, all of which lent specificity to the physical portrait of who she was. It was also important that she bustle about in an efficient manner as she hurried between Falstaff's sick room and her Inn, the Boar's Head Tavern. My shoes were a felted-wool slipper over thick stockings and I experimented with how she might best walk in them, padding about quickly and climbing on and off the enormous bed but it wasn't until I turned my feet out in 'first position', harkening back to my ballet days, that Nell was in the room. I felt the character climbing into me and affecting a freedom to speak and react from a physical reality completely unlike my own, liberating and honest as I veered from the high comedic moments to grief.

Method externalism is a term Andy and I have used, somewhat jokingly over the years, to describe this tool for character development. Sometimes it is essential to slowly climb into the character's skin as you examine psychological motivations and relate them to your own experience, playing somewhere along the lines of Stanislavski's Method. Or sometimes you can make an external choice like Nell's full figure and turned-out feet and you're off to the races.

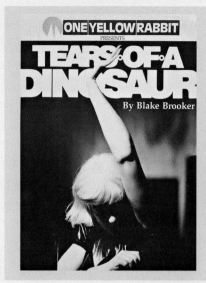

TEARS OF A DINOSAUR

"She was in the flush of her power. Everything watchable."
— Blake Brooker

One of my personal drives within the Lab has been this active research on how to guide the group through kinetic ideas and commands so that the physical work seems logical and practical, is adaptable for everyone, and leads to consciousness of the body in their own art making. In terms of additional techniques, I experimented with yoga, slowly incorporating the poses or asanas with my other kinetic pedagogies.

In 1997, yoga was nowhere near as ubiquitous as it is now and many Labbits (a name they chose themselves one year that seems to have stuck) had very little exposure to it. By this writing in 2018 it is quite normal for them to have some experience and knowledge of the form.

I have been a student of the art and science of yoga for most of my career because I so value the logic and sequence of both the philosophy and the asanas as my own tools for longevity and well-being. I also know that if a participant wants to continue developing their own practice once they leave the Lab, they can't go wrong looking up a good Hatha Yoga teacher. Hatha is Sanskrit for effort or force but has come to refer to the distinct study of one yoga pose at a time as opposed to the linked or flow style that privileges the workout over the technique.

Something else I appreciated was that by providing a yoga mat with the individual's name written on it, a small personal space was defined and in an interesting non-verbal way, signaled privacy for that individual. I had a great desire to give the Labbits each a sense of specific individuated study while we were together, hoping passionately that they would absorb this notion of their own physical **specificity** through **practice** and **repetition**, into their work.

This, of course, is my own bias, shared by the OYR Ensemble; a belief that onstage, **'everything is watchable'**, borrowed from Blake Brooker's 1988 play *Tears Of A Dinosaur*. My character, Liz lies on a table while her husband Roy places dozens of tiny dinosaurs all over her, turning her body into the Badlands, and recites the story of his early lust for her. The speech begins: "She was in the flush of her power. Everything watchable." **"Everything watchable"** grew to become a kind of understanding we shared that there was nothing happening on a stage that should be disregarded as insignificant because indeed the audience is capable of seeing everything. It inspired our highly specific physical style of theatre and affected much of how we built work including our passion for carefully choreographing even the transitions, which we saw as golden staging opportunities. Indeed we coined our own verb 'to **transish**'.

Chapter Three

PREFERENCES

It is common to refer to the collected skills in the artist's arsenal as their tool kit and clearly, the choice for most would be to stock that tool chest with all kinds of diverse and useful tools and develop the know-how to put them to use. As discussed in the previous chapter, by turning one's attention to a **postural preference,** one gathers self-knowledge and may opt to aim at correcting any misalignment in order to lessen the potential for injuries and/or to expand their opportunities to move in new ways; it's just one more tool to have in your kit. Applying that tool beyond posture and undergoing an examination and inventory of various **aesthetic and personal preferences**, is a profoundly effective tool for creative investigation. Once you have named those preferences, you are less likely to 'fall back' on them out of habit, resulting in liberating breakthroughs.

But as essential as it is to not put a value judgment on your own or other's posture, the same applies to your **personal preferences**, which are often your strengths, providing structure and starting points. This research is about expanding on what you have and giving you more options to **play** with, not to say that your habits and preferences are bad.

Let's look at a situation in a traditional theatre setting; an actor has become a 'type', perhaps it's the comedic type or the warm and affable type, the romantic lead type. They have a stockpile of techniques that serve them admirably, including vocal preferences, postures, and ways to establish that character. Now they are playing a complex murderous villain. The actor who has spent some time examining personal preferences, (some people refer to it as their 'bag of tricks' or their 'schtick'), has the knowledge they need to try new things in a whole new way.

It doesn't have to be a full makeover for the player to tap into a different posture or a new way of walking, or talking; it could be a subtle and nuanced shift. In the most terrifying psycho drama or the broadest comedy, the player who can find subtle distinction and variance is better able to convince the viewer, and theatre is about convincing the audience that although they are attending a made-up event, the characters are real enough to invest in and stay with because they have integrity and believability. The most gifted clown in the most outrageously funny work is still connecting on an authentic level while winking at the crowd that they understand it's all a play.

Deep and Available

The beauty of borrowing from Laban's vocabulary is that, like yoga, it is an available field to delve deeply into should the practitioner want to. The terms and elements are useful to either describe or generate movement and it is possible to use the terms already discussed to do both; creating studies that examine how your movement relates to your externalized self in the world. The language used by Laban scholars and practitioners is radical in the way that it privileges the transformative experience of a person moving in space over theory. A brief examination on-line will yield such concepts as 'whole person' education, whereby the learner is the active agent in their own empowered learning, rather than being a passive recipient of received language. Laban Movement Analysis (LMA) also speaks to the understanding of relationships between individuals, groups and societies. This is tremendously appealing to the performance theatre creator searching for their individual identity and voice in relationship to their collaborators/group, and to their audience/society.

Embracing the question posed at the beginning of this book, "Who are you now?" has led to the suggestion that you set up your Laboratory and begin the research and investigation of yourself in stillness, breathing, moving up and down the vertical and horizontal lines, proceeding into three-dimensional space and playing in space, whatever that means to you. The dancer will be familiar with all of these notions, as will, one would hope, the actor trained in a theatre school, with the writer or the director perhaps slightly less so. It may be necessary to encourage and remind all performance theatre creators that their body is part of their creative process and to deny movement may inhibit progress. Or not. It would be optimal to experience it oneself, but to the creator uninterested in performing one's own work, or if moving one's own body is out of the question, applying these ideas to observing other people is also invaluable.

To review
- **Shape Flow** is amoeba-like movement that originates from the core and is 'limb-less'. Think paramecium moving on the microscope slide, or 'grooving' at the nightclub while you look around, or, once you've enjoyed a few too many, think drunk person swaying.
- **Carving** is curvilinear, flowing movement within spherical dimensions. Think of your arms or hips

painting a 'figure 8' in space. Think of figure skating, or the modern dancer spiralling up and down from the floor.
- **Directional** movement is what Laban called movements with the limbs moving outward on a straight line, spoke like, to a finite spot. Think baseball, ballet, hurdles, handshakes or the little kid in a starfish position demonstrating how big they are.
- In her book *Making Connections*, the LMA artist Peggy Hackney says,

Each human being combines these movement factors in his/her own unique way and organizes them to create phrases and relationships which reveal personal, artistic or cultural style.[1]

Observation of Others

Let us turn our attention to the observation of others and use these three 'lenses of movement' categories to describe what you see. No value judgments please, just observe, analyze, and describe.

It's a dance party and Prince is the soundtrack. A person is listening, grooving with small undulations from the core of their body, which allows them to enjoy the music and watch people on the dance floor, or across the room, from inside their somewhat small kinesphere. It could be that this person is just warming up and checking out the scene, but if after a few hours they maintain the small groove/sway you could describe them as having a preference for shape flow movement. Myriad questions arise as to what keeps someone grooving on the sidelines in this relatively uncommitted way. Did they decide to move this way or is it just the way they interact at a dance party? Is

---

1   Peggy Hackney. *Making Connections: Total Body Integration Through Bartenieff Fundamentals.* Philadelphia: Gordon & Breach, 1997.

*The Lab: Practicing directional movement.
An investigation of self by setting up one's private Lab.*

it because they are extremely cool? Or shy? Do they think they are not good dancers? Do they dislike funk music? If this person is you, then apply this lens broadly to yourself.

Do you prefer shape flow movement in other situations as well? At work or in rehearsal are you an observer who waits and watches, collecting data and biding your time while others hold the floor? Is it a strategy to use small movement that does not draw the eye while plotting your best move? With this lens on yourself you might identify a mere tendency or a strong preference but either way it's informative to your creative work. If we use the lens/tool to examine what this preference says about us, or those we work with, culturally and aesthetically, we gain an appreciation and understanding of personal differences, all of which will help to balance a creative workroom. Collaboration with an entire posse of folks with a **shape**

flow preference might be tricky to work with, but so might the opposite: a room full of **directional** preference! Let's have a look.

Same dance party, and a person is on the floor exuberantly punching out the beat, jumping up and down and hollering joyfully to friends. They lift both arms in celebration and generally perform large locomotor movement using lots of space. Possibly even too much space because sometimes they jostle against others but it is a committed body in motion, eager to express rhythm and suggests that this is a person who is having fun and who likes to be in the action not just observing it. The exuberance of **directional** movement is hard to miss and begs a host of other questions. Are they drunk or just happy to be dancing to Prince? Do they care that people are watching them or do they ignore that and give themselves to the social occasion unselfconsciously? If it's you, the answers to these questions might leap out or it may surprise you to see yourself in this way. Ask yourself if you have a general tendency to move directionally. Are you the person who strides across the space boldly, hand outstretched to meet or greet another person? Do you use deliberate eye focus, follow through with a firm handshake, and speak in a similarly direct manner? Do you often put others at ease, breaking the ice and getting things started, or are you occasionally startled to realize you are overwhelming a situation with your full-scale manner?

Just as the room of laid-back collaborators leaning into the **shape flow** tendency might be hard, so would the big, bold gang of **directional** movers be. But it's a folly to assume that a preference for one extreme or another, **shape flow vs directional** describes you all the time in every situation. Of course that is not the case. Everyone moves in all these ways. You may discover that you are a quiet and contained person but that sometimes you just love to break out your moves and get big on the dance floor. To ask yourself what circumstances or cultural conditions motivate you is a study that may provide golden information about you and your personal preferences in relation to others in the world.

Fascinating then, to think about the individual on the dance floor **carving** space. They are smooth to observe and seem to be molding themselves around the ambient movement. They shrink their kinesphere or expand it, accommodating both the still folks and the big locomotors. They don't jostle others, even in motion, they seem aware of their surroundings and able to express themselves while they stay out of the way of the other Prince fans. So is this person 'the fixer' in their everyday life? Smoothing out the angles and corners for greater ease in the workroom too? Do they over-accommodate and carve their way right out of making their own point? Or are they a beloved asset in any process cooperating with everyone and inviting attention only when necessary?

For a director, it could be easier to help an actor in these terms. If a scene is not working and the director can see that the actor is relying on a preference, for example shrinking themselves and devaluing vocally, when the director wants to see it played with more direct emotional lines, it may be difficult to simply ask the actor to **'bigger it up'**. Just as tough will be asking the consistently bold and direct player to try a smaller more nuanced approach. It's easy to demoralize or embarrass them and can lead beyond questions of motivation and mess with their personal psychology. With the vocabulary of **Directional vs Shape Flow vs Carving,** the onus is not to presume the actor's psychological state but to give them something active to play, physically leaving the job of acting up to them. The same applies to the writer who has opted to explore all three ways of moving, they may find they can transfer their discoveries to the page and see how their own preferences are affecting plot or dialogue or look at their cast of characters through the lenses which could affect their action.

This notion of observing and analyzing movement as a method for better understanding personal preference and applying it to the creative workroom extends beyond the purely artistic realm suggested here. An LMA practitioner named Warren Lamb (1923–2014) was a movement consultant who studied under Laban and went on to develop his own system called Movement Pattern Analysis. He used his system to recruit management teams for multinational corporations identifying movement patterns as predictors of how people will react in various situations. The method proved to be so successful that the US government brought him on to create profiles of foreign leaders. Recently, researchers from Harvard University conducted a fascinating study of MPA to research the unique advantages of "observational methods for deciphering telling indicators of decision-making style," as they put it.

What will become obvious when using the three LMA tools suggested here, for observing yourself and other people, is that it is easy to make value judgments. But this specific use of LMA is *not* a way of nailing character assessment or defining yourself and others in absolute terms. It isn't a good or bad tendency to live in a physically direct manner, or to always carve space for others, or to prefer shaping your actions internally. Used as one more tool, this process of movement analysis privileges the body experience equally to the intellectual and psychological aspects of creative experimentation and investigation, and perhaps helps to address imbalances in an individual or a group that threaten the ongoing ability to work together. The study of your personal movement preferences opens a window onto examining other preferences, aesthetic and cultural, furthering your understanding of 'who you are now' and how you roll. Self-knowledge lends compassion and respect to how you view others in various situations, an advantage to you as a person and as an artist and to the art you make.

Activity PLAY
*Set yourself a timer for five minutes and move **directionally** the whole time. Repeat it moving in **shape flow**, and then **carve** for five more minutes. Play back and forth for shorter and shorter increments. Perform these five minutes studies over a period of a few weeks or longer and bring your attention to whether or not you enjoy one way of moving more than another. Try it in silence and with music. Do it alone or invite pals. Add it to your warm-up or try it at a nightclub.*

Add these questions to your research and study.

Does it feel as though your preference in the directed study above matches the way you interact at work and socially?

The way you talk and ask questions?

Is it connected to your mood?

If you are using various musical choices, do they change your preference?

Does your preference change as the weeks pass and your awareness of it grows?

Can you see movement preferences in your colleagues, friends and family?

Are you being generous to yourself and others as you conduct this study, or do you find yourself judging one as a superior trait?

ONE YELLOW RABBIT

"OH GOOD," THEY SAID, "YOU SING IT."
— THE RABBITS

I trained as a ballet dancer my entire young life and invested totally in the form and the aesthetic. At seventeen years of age I found myself in the pre-professional training program at the Royal Winnipeg Ballet. Included in our training was a jazz dance class, and I was suddenly asked to place my feet in a parallel position and to move my pelvis in a whole new way.

I found the dropping of my centre of gravity into the earth, the conscious isolated movements that stretched the plane of the torso into trapezoids and the generally relaxed style of dance completely embarrassing. Although I loved social dancing, I was frozen by the sensuality of what was being asked of me. It meant abandoning my familiar modes of expression and as a kid who was a hundred percent committed to the life and the culture of the ballet world, that was extremely difficult. But the teacher was fun and very cool and one day told me I had the makings of a good jazz dancer. Naturally I was encouraged and the classes grew to be tremendously enjoyable. I relaxed, and my skills added up so much so that I went from Winnipeg to Montreal to apprentice with Les Ballets Jazz the following year and worked on CBC television as a show dancer, which most definitely drew on the jazz idiom.

Eventually I realized I was more interested in making my own dances and developing my own style and I began exploring modern dancers and the contemporary dance world. Right away I had an aversion to it but this time I found myself not so much frozen in mortification as I was insouciant and filled with a kind of dismissive attitude towards that kind of movement.

It wasn't until I met a young professor of modern dance named Anne Flynn at the University of Calgary, where I had begun to teach, that my clouded perceptions towards the culture and style of contemporary dance began to shift. We began to make dances together, marrying techniques and ideologies of dance aesthetics and pedagogies into our own thing. I am indebted to Anne for introducing me to the somatic body workers I have outlined and it was a radical change that began to influence me away from my prejudices and biases towards a greater understanding of how all movement is beautiful and useful to draw on. It allowed me to learn how to use my technique to serve me rather than the other way around. I saw how I could combine the kinetic information I had

With Anne Flynn in the mid-eighties.

amassed my entire life and make something new both as a soloist and a choreographer of new dance and theatre.

And then one day, my freaky friends in the theatre asked me to perform in their brand new company called One Yellow Rabbit. It was a non-verbal role and I was completely at ease with it until one day when they were searching for a way to sing a poem and I blurted out a way it could be sung. "Oh good", they said, "you sing it." I remember almost fainting because I was a dancer, I did not use my voice! But I accepted that invitation and once again the culture, style and expectations of the theatre world shifted everything for me aesthetically.

I come up against my own preferences repeatedly as a writer, a director, a choreographer and an actor. Leaning into a decidedly directional tendency, I have learned to modify my vocal habit of 'pushing' within the line for emphasis. How to mix it up, from the boldly physical to subtle nuanced choices when designing the character's physicality. How to play with dynamic intensity and keep the audience surprised and engaged. The investigation never ends and I am grateful for the tools that help me to remain a servant of the art that sustains me.

Chapter Four

CREATING PERSONAL VOCABS AND REPETITION

You have begun active personal research to explore your **aesthetic preferences**, designed and engaged in a **practice** and are now moving towards creating your heart's desire. Presuming that you have also chosen one or a few desired elements: a motivating concept, colleagues, musical ideas, technological or set pieces – it doesn't really matter what those elements are for you to commence activity – the questions can swirl once again as to how to begin generating material for the stage. Often, the spoken text begins to take precedence and priority. To write a play is its own art form and demands its own process, which this book only presumes to speak about, with the hope that many of the notions suggested might be helpful to the playwright.

Performance theatre most certainly does not preclude working with an existing play, but it does place a premium on who will perform that play. Furthermore, it honours the physicality of the players throughout the rehearsal process. Traditional theatre-makers tend to focus on table work; readings and analysis to begin, followed only later by getting 'on their feet' and blocking the play. Tight schedules determine most of the day's activity – investing in the artists' preparation and physical explorations is a luxury most traditional, professional theatres do not feel they can afford. But long days sitting around a table, hammering out meaning and listening, can be exhausting, and the effect on the group can be mounting stress or boredom. To schedule time for the company to feel their bodies moving, might be considered radical and/or 'wanky' unless one remembers that these are the bodies that will be onstage performing as an ensemble, **playing the play**. To invest in time to breathe and move together every day could better be considered a big secret weapon. This secret weapon is also a practical and useful part of the work with the ante going up considerably if the desire is to include a strong physicality in the final product, which is the presumption here.

When devising physical performance theatre, be it a solo project or an ensemble creation, a large part is, of course, story and text generation. But mutually beneficial to the spoken and written elements will be the concurrent invention and execution of related **physical vocabularies. Everything is watchable** and the players are the delivery system of that viewing experience.

If they are to perform physical elements, then the more they repeat those elements the more watchable they will be and the greater the opportunity for virtuosity. Daily repetition equals precision and precision equals relaxation. It's a *cadeau* or gift for the player, and ultimately for the audience.

What are **physical vocabularies**? Possibly a choreographer is responsible, but without choreographic training, it may be daunting to think about the larger physicality of a project – even with choreographic training, physicality can be daunting. **Personal vocabularies** are an excellent tool to begin with, breaking down bigger concepts into distinct studies. Right away, there is something immediately active in the room and the players are playing. Treat these studies like any other aspect or element to add and arrange on what

VOCABULARIES 55

The Lab: Makambe K. Simamba performing "Our Fathers, Sons, Lovers ... Brothers." Expressing specific physicality and personal vocabulary.

Leonard Cohen called "your arborite table."

A **personal vocabulary** or **vocab** is a phrase of gestural movement; think sign language combined with 'vogueing', that provides the player with an opportunity to make a physical study of the character they will play. It is best approached from inside the kinesphere, in a somewhat planted place, which surprisingly is a limitation that quickly becomes an engine for movement invention. There is a universe of movement to choose from inside the kinesphere. To deal with the larger spatial relationship is that much more intimidating.

The player might feel foolish or embarrassed expressing themselves emotionally and a common response is to immediately judge each physical choice as unappealing or lame. The kinesphere is slightly safer because it gives the artist the privacy they need and is a manageable scale. (They also have to flip the switch, and **stop judging**.)

Specificity is the mother of all secret weapons for the stage. Having the control to use the body in space with specificity yields big rewards for the player and the viewer – even proponents of chaotic mayhem do it best when it's organized chaos. Like a monologue that reveals deeper meaning with each day of rehearsal, the **vocab** that gets repeated a hundred times can take the player towards virtuosic territory. As they become more confident they can speed it up, slow it down, do it standing, sitting, rhythmically, or abstractly. They can bust it directionally on a beat, like they are 'voguing' (see the film *Paris Is Burning*) or carve it lyrically while repeating text. They can shrink it to a subtle hand dance, barely referring to its original scale, or bigger it up into a cartoon. The **personal vocab** serves as a non-verbal portrait of their character, framed by the membrane of the **kinesphere**. Adding the enlarged spatial element will take away that **framing device**, however once the player is completely fluent with the vocab, the ability to attach it to big motor pathway movement is made that much more possible.

The first step is to create a prompt document to refer to so that the gestural choices relate to the bigger project and specifically to who you are and who you want to play. Perhaps best to approach this as though a process is in place and a performance creation is beginning.

Activity PLAY
Let's imagine a creative posse of five players and a director. They've decided to make an urban hip-hop Sleeping Beauty *and the cast of characters includes the hibernating Princess, the Prince who will wake her, an Evil Fairy, a Good Fairy and a Narrator. The team gathers their elements: an extant version of the Grimm's fairytale, a list of actions, descriptions and intentions of each character's 'journey' through the story, an iconic song. The plan is to hammer out basic story lines, scene and*

song concepts and also to commit to an hour or two a day of physical work. They agree to start with **personal vocabs** and so they'll need to make a **prompt document**. It could be drawn from any of the elements but let's say in this case, a fill-in-the-blank character questionnaire is invented, designed to reveal information about their back stories:

1. My name is __(your character's name)_____.
2. I am _____ years old.
3. I live in _____.
4. _____makes me laugh.
5. My favourite activity is_____.
6. My favourite video game is _____.
7. My best friend is _____.
8. My worst enemy is _____.
9. The worst thing that ever happened to me is _____.
10. My future looks like this:_____.

The sky is the limit and even choosing the prompts can be invigoratingly active. There is no perfect number but the longer the list, the longer it will take to make the **vocab**, so ten prompts is ideal.

The players write down their answers and armed with the document, they find a private spot to plant themselves and begin to assign one gesture per prompt, moving through the list until they have a phrase of ten movements that they can remember and repeat. It's all totally up to the player and the gestures can dance between mime and abstract flourishes, change tempos and levels, use any range of movement from the most subtle to the grandest but for now should stay in one spot.

If they move with a playful kind of first-blink approach, choosing the movement fairly quickly and intuitively like a painter doing pencil sketches before committing to paint, they run less of a risk of bogging down. This work is light and not labour intensive although it isn't easy. It can be hard to remember movement for even the seasoned pro, and although this can be a lot of fun, it might also feel boring to repeat the same ten moves over and over, but the rigour and discipline involved has its benefits. Each repetition increases specificity and detail. The individual grows more articulate and fluent; they move with an increasingly informed narrative and the payoff is that they become marvelously watchable.

One or two days into the process, the Sleeping Beauty group has generated five physical elements, they have learned something about the characters and their back-stories, they can examine personal movement preferences and they are using the intuitive body in an active and playful way. The director and choreographer can either participate or observe these portraits and gains useable information about both the player and the physicality of their character. If each player teaches their phrase to the group, there is the possibility of having generated a substantial chunk of choreographic language that can have any intention or imperative placed on it: slow motion as a beautiful or terrifying dream sequence, mechanically beat to beat as a banquet tableaux, innocently to invoke a carefree childhood, you get the idea.

The exercise can continue with the posse generating various vocabularies or serve only as a beginning study, but either way it is valuable time well spent. Just as the actor believes that the single most important technique for speaking their text is to know it inside out and sideways, so does the physical theatre-maker realize that movement repeated until it is second nature, reveals similar meaning and potential. What began life as a bunch of random gestural responses to some statements becomes a precise and economical expression because even the fastest sketch by an untrained mover will grow magically from the **generalized** to the **specific** and become utterly unique and engaging to watch.

Photos: Mike Tan, Diane + Mike Photography

WHAT THE THUNDER SAID

The OYR show *What The Thunder Said*, is a triptych with scene one setting the context, a second scene ballet macabre to Led Zeppelin's *Kashmir*, and T. S. Eliot's *The Wasteland* as the third panel of the piece. Blake Brooker directed and Andy Curtis, Michael Green, and Peter Hinton joined me to create and perform.

Andy, Michael, and Peter are gifted actors but none of them would describe themselves as dancers, yet we committed to this notion of a ballet macabre. To make relevant movement choices it was decided that the four of us would assign one gesture to each of the 433 lines of *The Wasteland*. We moved very quickly, retreating every four lines to invent the next moves, one each, before reconvening and teaching them, adding one line after the other, constantly reviewing our sequencing then soldiering on. I say 'soldiering on' because it was extremely rigorous and repetitive work but after one week we had a physical language that stood on its own as the choreographic base of the ballet macabre which I then set for us to the Led Zeppelin. My non-dancer comrades moved elegantly through the eight-and-a-half-minute 'ballet', striding in and out of the light and delivering their movement with power and authority.

The movement looked good, and it made sense to us because we had constructed it directly in relation to the themes and language of the Eliot poem; the social cultural wasteland after the death and destruction of the First World War. I rely on this method of movement invention for the way it empowers actors to move whether or not they have dance training. It definitely speaks to my own **aesthetics,** but years of experience have taught me it can be adapted to anyone's **preference** and played with qualitatively so that it works for everyone in the room.

CABARET

**WILLKOMMEN! BIENVENUE! WELCOME!
FREMDER, ÉTRANGER, STRANGER.**

Creating personal vocabs is useful in all kinds of theatrical settings. Besides my long association with One Yellow Rabbit and my solo work, I work as a choreographer of musicals and operas. I have enjoyed a career spanning relationship with the brilliant Canadian director Peter Hinton and in 2014 he invited me to choreograph his production of *Cabaret* for the Shaw Festival. It's a musical that has been done many, many times in many cities.

I had done the show before but Peter had a strong take on it and I was inspired to approach the material again because I so enjoy how he creates his rehearsal room. He does vast amounts of research, posting illustrations, photos and reproductions of significant art work on all the walls and paints the world of the play politically, socially, and culturally in his articulate first day speeches preceding the read through. We decided that for the artists of the Shaw Festival to have a whole new entry point for their roles, we would start right in on day two with the creation of personal vocabs. I knew that these were more traditionally practiced actors so I was delighted when they responded to the idea enthusiastically.

Cabaret is a fascinating vehicle, loaded with tremendously dynamic musical numbers, featuring the seedy denizens of the Kit Kat Klub. At the same time it tells two tender love stories unfolding against a terrifying backdrop as Hitler's Germany replaces the hedonistic excesses of Berlin during the Weimar days.

Because of the non-binary nature of many of the characters and the familiar tone of German cabaret of the time, the show can fall into a campy place. Instead, we were intrigued by the idea of presenting our audience with who those cabaret artists really were, in and out of the club, and revealing their individuality even as they performed the tremendously appealing ensemble show tunes. The MC introduces them by name in the opening song, Wilkommen and gives a very brief description of each of them. Those names were our starting point and I designed a personal prompt profile.

Personal Prompt Profile

I am _____
When I was born, my mother was _____ and my father was _____.
After WW1, our family _____.
We came to Berlin because _____.
I love _____ and _____.
I always _____ and _____ but I never _____.
The only thing I've ever needed was _____.
I hate _____.
One day I will _____ but I will never _____.

The company took a half hour or so to think about and fill in those blanks before moving into private spots and beginning to assign gestures. In minutes the room was a hive of unbelievable movement invention, utterly unique portraits coming to life in every kinesphere. The written questionnaire remained private to each actor but the resulting physical portrait revealed a rich tapestry of varied character detail in vivid nonverbal terms.

The actors understood that I would be borrowing from them and rearranging their vocabs here and there throughout the show but for *Wilkommen* we featured each artist busting out their own in a spectacle of wild, weird, and wonderful that set the tone for the night. They were magnificently authentic and amazing to watch. With many weeks of rehearsal under their belts the vocabs had stretched and shape-shifted into dazzling precision, performed with powerful, grounded relaxation that introduced the cast as fascinating individuals rather than as stock characters in similar costumes blurring into the amorphous 'Kit Kat boys and girls'. They carried this personal detail into the entire story, populating our Berlin with a segment of a society facing the complex horror and pathos of annihilation, which helped make Peter's production the beautifully dark, emotional epic that it was.

I use personal vocabs much as a musical arranger might use musical phrases. If each player constructs a vocab/phrase using a document like the one we used for *Cabaret* with fourteen prompts, the phrase is a surprisingly substantial one. Depending on how familiar the actor is with remembering movement, and how long your creation period is, a vocab can be as long as you want and with repetition it will become more and more precise, coherent and watchable.

Chapter Five

PRECISION, ECONOMY, AND RELAXATION

Throughout the preceding chapters, you will have noted the regular appearance of these three words: **Precision. Economy. Relaxation.** They are a constant touch point in the One Yellow Rabbit working vocabulary and something the ensemble reminds itself of throughout the rehearsal period and before every performance. As a young man, Blake Brooker defined this exceptionally concise triadic mantra for himself and for the other bunch of punks who made up the OYR ensemble, as words to live by when making shows. Eventually the mantra was included in those 21st century things called mandates and vision statements, which funding bodies and boards appreciate – but these words have never deteriorated to a mere slogan.

To sum up a theatre company's aesthetic principle in three words is impossible, but precision, economy, and relaxation are evident in every aspect of our work. From the office team, who produce and administer all theatrical endeavor, to the assembled artists, to the final product on the stage, there has always been a commitment to all three of those words. It became a constant reminder that while nobody can predict if a show will be deemed 'good', it can be constructed to be **undeniable**: the work onstage is authentic, **precise** and true to its own **economy** of scale, balancing dynamics, information and emotion in an engaging way, delivered by actors who appear **relaxed** and confident. It may or may not be to every viewer's taste, but it is **undeniably** well made and performed.

The mantra has held OYR in good philosophical stead, helping to carry on the original goal of creating a body of work that would withstand scrutiny and the test of time for as long as the ensemble cared to continue.

Precision

The goal of repetition is to become **precise**. Not rote. **Precise**. The best argument *against* too much repetition might be that the emotional verity of the character is in danger of being drummed out and the playing made mechanical and deadly. Of course, it is a consideration.

Some film actors and directors advocate for only the bare minimum of rehearsal in service of on screen naturalism, which makes sense knowing the camera's merciless eye for 'fake'. French film theorist and critic André Bazin, for example, identified cinema as a fulfillment of the human craving for realistic representation.

Certainly in films that strive for naturalism and realism, it is understandable that a bias against overly precise performances might exist. The new film movement of the 1950s and 60s was a revolt against the conventional elitism of the previous era; the choreographed glamorous façade of Hollywood and especially the highly stylized German expressionist films, which became equated with fascism and totalitarianism. Suddenly naturalism and realism were the vogue and we see the influence to this day in the majority of filmmaking.

Theatre is a very different beast, or is it? In his book, *Antigone Undone: Juliet Binoche, Anne Carson, Ivo van*

Hove, and The Art of Resistance,[1] author Will Aitken describes his experience of watching the French film star, Juliet Binoche in rehearsal for the theatre production of Anne Carson's translation of *Antigone*, directed by Ivo Van Hove. He compares her work during the dress rehearsals

> She doesn't have it all worked out ... she may not even know what she is going to do next. All free fall and danger.

to that of the British cast who

> ... glide about her, perfect in word and deed, as if some time ago they'd all decided how their performances would go.

It seems at first that Aitken is entranced by Binoche and feels that although inconsistent, she is conveying superior emotional power to the British actors who clearly know what they are doing. In subsequent performances, however, he is deeply impressed when he sees the two styles come together so that the entire company is working together to deliver Antigone's wild story with focus and control.

There is another advantage that **precision** delivers to its adherents, most especially in the world of collective theatre-making where there is more than one healthy ego at play. The bonus is a **generous** room observing full **etiquette**. The **precision** that develops with repetition means you are on top of your memory work as much as anything, which is the customary rule of thumb in theatre. **Etiquette** is a fussy word, but if everyone has to speak text and play

---

[1] Will Aitken. *Antigone Undone: Juliet Binoche, Anne Carson, Ivo van Hove, and the Art of Resistance.* Regina: University of Regina, 2018.

scenes with one another, especially with big emotional stakes, it goes better when all the players have learned their lines and remember their movement.

Even in the most punk rooms, it's a drag on the available energy if one or more of the posse is consistently behind. This is not to say there is no space for error, indeed rehearsal is where you fail over and over until you don't, but even the most **generous** room full of compassion and respect is tested by having to stop or wait for the same reason too many times. It's a fine balance and neither way is the right way or the only way, nor are they mutually exclusive. Why not save the argument and agree on excellence, moving as steadily as possible towards precision while remaining lively and available to play, and encouraging forward momentum?

Economy
Less is more. One Yellow Rabbit happens to favour minimalism as the overriding staging and playing aesthetic, from the big elements like sets and costumes to the tiny ones like shuffling of feet to the beating of heads, and flapping of hands. (Commit to memory Leonard Cohen's, *How To Speak Poetry* and you too may be forever changed.)

Beyond just a proclivity for minimalism though, '**economy**' means a careful management of available resources. An inventory of resources available for any theatrical endeavor might include:

1. Money
2. Time
3. Space
4. Energy
5. Ambition
6. Ability

The Lab: Andrew Barrett performs "Paper Bag Prince."

You may add or subtract from this list of resources, but the point is that they are all finite and it's wise to ensure that they are well allocated. All of these could be understood as overlapping 'commodities' that affect each other, and the balance and distribution of them from beginning to end, describe the **economy** of your project. It's helpful if everyone understands that **economy** through the macro lens or the big picture, but also on the micro or personal level.

1. Money

Understanding that the producing team cannot spend more money than is in the budget is obvious although budgets get over-run all the time, a serious flaw if the goal is sustainability. The big picture here is that the producers simply cannot do that, but neither can the individual player. In spite of the less-than-lavish pay cheque that most theatre gigs can offer, spend your money wisely and look after yourself so you can show up for work rested, fed and ready to rock.

2. Time

The hours in the day, multiplied by the days in the week, and by the weeks you have contracted, will make it evident that time really is a precious commodity, because there is rarely enough of it. Here is where the Stage Manager shines. In particular, when it's a massive show with a huge cast and hundreds of cues to record, it's the gifted SM who runs things with full attention to the schedule while maintaining a graceful handle on when it needs to shift to accommodate the needs of the production.

In the more intimate practice that a company like OYR enjoys, the SM is part of the creative stream of activity and respects that there is a shorthand and a style that includes silliness, mischief, and laughter. What might appear like time wasted is actually how the group likes to work, and so it is part of the schedule. However it's up to each ensemble member to also keep an eye on how they use their personal time and to respect deadlines as a necessary evil.

3. Space

Space might seem like a pretty straightforward element of the **economy** of the project. There is the physical room you need to make the show and the theatre to perform it in, but on the micro plane there is also the psychic space, that is, the personal space that the creators need. For example: during the break, you need to discuss something but the director is deep in thought, problem solving or just recharging their psychic battery. Ask yourself if you can hold off and give them the twenty minutes they need. Conversely for the director, gauging how much individual space is necessary for a player depends on the nature of their role. An intense drama could charge the atmosphere differently than a rip-snorting comedy, and they must read how the inner emotional life of the character and the action is affecting the player. 'Space' is a big part of what is referred to as a 'safe working place' in today's parlance and a welcome addition to the theatre language it is. The artist who feels emotionally comfortable and respected is bound to look twice at others with the same focus and as the quality of engagement goes up, so does the freedom to dig deep and find authentic emotional expression.

4. Energy

Energy is a commodity that can actually run out – as serious a problem as having no money, time, or space. The macro view is that a project has its own energy measurable in the vibrancy of the players. This includes their vision and their 'timeliness' – some things just seem meant to be and come blasting into the scene while others are brought carefully and slowly to life or never at all. But let's zoom in on the energy being spent in the rehearsal room as well as in the actual playing.

There is nothing more welcome than a gregarious and fun person keeping things buoyant during rehearsal, however on occasion it might be too much of a good thing. If that person is you, be respectful of when to give it a rest. The opposite holds true as well and if you bring a low energy mood to the room too often, you may have more effect than you know. If it is beyond a habit of mood and you are in real mental distress, then that is something to make known immediately to your SM and your director. Similarly a performance that revs at the same tempo, high or low, from beginning to end, vocally, physically or emotionally can be wearisome.

Take the time to analyze how you spend your personal energy in both rehearsal and in performance to keep things economical, dynamically balanced and engaging for your fellow players and for your audience.

5. Ambition

Ambition is a word that often gets a bad rap. There are many images alive in the popular culture of ambitious monsters clawing their way through the well-being of others to get what they want. It's not always a bad thing to be ambitious though. It's like an odor. Ambition to succeed at what you do, while bringing others along with you, is pleasant smelling. Personal drive at any cost stinks.

Aiming high while adding to the culture of a civil society is the job of all theatre artists, collectively and individually. But one person consistently striving to get out in front of others will bring ill will and dissonance to any endeavour. Stay ambitious and generous. Be your own brilliant artist and the best playing partner. It is an investment in good will and integrity, things you can trade in as you find your posse and your patrons. Plus, you will have a better time and your chances of building a strong body of work with great colleagues will accrue.

6. Ability

Ability is the sibling of talent and most definitely does not exclude persons with disabilities. Whatever your challenges, talent is what you're born with; ability is what you do with it. Sometimes talent is unleashed with ability. You may not know that you have lavish musical gifts until you learn how to play an instrument or sing. To fill your talent pool with ability is sort of an insurance policy for success.

Even if time, money and space are short, a mark can be made as a talented group or soloist when the ability on view is undeniable. When you invite a public to observe your work, it's always an opportunity to capture their imagination and make them curious as to what you'll do next, which is a big part of how an audience is built and how the **economy** of your theatrical endeavor can become more and more reliable.

Relaxation

Relaxation harkens back to the beginning of this book and returns us on a circular path to the whole point of having a practice and training the nervous system. It must not be construed as an admonition to approach things casually or without commitment. Nor is it something you can command, but you can create an atmosphere where a relaxed vibe can occur. Some folks are more nervous and tense than others, and so if the rehearsal room feels somewhat at ease, hopefully they can take a breath and bring their best game to the table.

"But theatre-making relies on creative tension," I hear someone exclaim. Stories abound of oil and water personality types who clash like titans at every turn, with fabulous results; standing ovations and teary hugs that make it all seem worthwhile. Maybe your particular brand of genius operates on that wavelength and needs that tightening of the creative screws. If that sounds like you, then hats off, but it's a tough way to live a life. Not to mention that theatre is a collaborative art form and it might be hard on those you want to work with. Even a soloist needs other people to get their work onto the stage. It's as though the macro is dependent on the micro. Remember this is how you are spending your time on earth. The whole posse has to agree, individually and as a group, to keep tensions at bay as best they can for the production to find its way without too much unpleasantness.

When Blake Brooker reminds the ensemble of **relaxation**, he is speaking in terms of **watchability** because it is his contention that a player who is tense repels the eye, which is intriguing for the actor to consider if they are playing a character who is tightly strung. There is good tension and bad tension. Dramatic tension is good. Performance tension is not. The viewer does not want to watch the player working too hard. It's like magic. Viewers want to be carried along in the illusion but if they can see all the mechanics of what you're doing, it wrecks that magic. To access the relaxed moment has an effect on the audience too and if you can let them lean back in their seats here and there, it's as though you refresh them before inviting them back into the action. It keeps the emotional life of the play alive and authentic, inspiring the audience to tap into their own deep currents, which is one of the reasons people come to the theatre.

The brilliant 20th century theatrical genius Noël Coward made the witty and astute observation,

> I will accept anything in the theatre … provided it amuses or moves me. But if it does neither, I want to go home.

Relaxed and authentic emotions, played with nuance, resonate with the audience and are one more secret to keeping them in their seats.

To Recap Part I The Player

The conscious player's tool kit:
1. Stop judging. The time for discernment will come but first you must begin the work.
2. Give yourself permission.
3. Design your practice from the palette of stillness.
4. Breathe and investigate relaxation techniques.
5. Scan and explore your posture and your personal space – your kinesphere.
6. Engage in serious physical play.
7. Examine Preferences.
8. Explore the use of Physical Vocabs.
9. Think about Precision, Economy and Relaxation on the macro and micro planes.

One could say that numbers one through four are all about making the decision to begin, moving from stillness through the nervous system and the skeleton with focus and **relaxation**.

Five through seven are like checking out the **economy** of you. Who are you? How do you stand, move, play? What are your strengths and/or weaknesses and how do you apply this information to your process?

Finally, eight and nine are techniques for the generation of physical performative materials and the **precision** it takes to present them to the public.

Using all the tools discussed so far, in balance and wellness, will aid you as you strive to give voice to what stirs and moves you as an artist. The negotiation and application of these tools will define you and give you the architecture necessary to house the artist's inner life providing succor and systems for dealing with what can, on occasion, feel like a lonely and hostile playing field.

Photo: Trudie Lee

WAG!

*"You are a weirdo and I don't know
what to think of you but goodbye now!"*

Feeling a hole in my creative self in the winter of 2012 after my oldest brother's death, I walked through the freezing white landscape of Prince's Island Park to the Big Secret Theatre. Things were quiet in the lull between late November rehearsals finishing and the start of OYR's annual festival, The High Performance Rodeo so the theatre sat empty and I snuck in each day to take advantage of the quiet and solitude. I had no budget but I had time, space, and ability. I had the energy of grief, which is a lonely kind of thing and my only ambition was to transform it into something that might soothe me. A few days passed listlessly attempting to find solace in music and free movement, or improvising and videoing random physical phrases and monologues but nothing was actually helping. Finally I sat down in a heap and after a good cry, resolved to put my faith in **my practice** and at least move steadily through breath and yoga and meditation to calm myself before trudging back home in the cold December twilight. The practice inspired me to one more action and before I packed up to go home, I decided to take note of all the elements I felt at play in me. I found my big coloured Post-its and made an inventory of the various monologue bits, ideas, music and **vocabs** I might be able to work with.

The next day as I returned once again through the silent park, I realized that I felt a bit better. Standing in the middle of the exquisite untouched snow by myself, in my giant parka and heavy winter boots, I was seized by the desire to muck up that perfect snow scape. The previous day's Post-it inventory search had reminded me of an unused physical vocab and I plowed into the middle of the field and started doing it. It was very silly but I thoroughly enjoyed myself until I noticed a bewildered dog, tail wagging and then not, and its humans watching, so I hurriedly wrapped it up, waved to them and continued in the opposite direction to the theatre. Behind me the dog barked excitedly as though to say; "You are a weirdo and I don't know what to think of you but goodbye now!"

Inside the space, still in my parka and boots, back pack on my back, laughing my ass off at how ridiculous I must have looked to the couple and their dog, I followed the urge to recreate the nonsense in the park and repeated the vocab bundled in the heavy clothing. Something broke through my sadness as I played, breathing and laughing and getting very warm in my down coat and boots. The experience became the opening scene of my solo *Wag!*, named for the way dogs can't help but show their feelings.

Each day for the remainder of the time I had, I followed my practice into physical studies and writing sessions, cueing off the Post-its until I had an hour plus of performative stuff and then began connecting and honing things with experiments and repetitions. There was no firm plan but the combination of rigorous repetition and intuitive play generated a sad/funny narrative that finally began to soothe the sorrow that had flattened me for months.

A Fabulous Disaster

Photo: Sean Dennie

It was clear that one of my goals was to steer around sticky sentimentality towards the more universal experience each of us feels when we confront death. As each element came into focus or fell away, the expression became more theatrical and playful until I felt sufficiently confident that I could move and amuse an audience with what I was doing.

I perhaps risked a little too much repetition when I decided to make a physical vocab prompted by a list of 114 books that I had used a few years previously in my solo piece, *A Fabulous Disaster*. In that show my heartbroken character recited every book title from the shelf of mingled books once shared in a marriage that had ended. I had never intended for the list to stay in the final draft but, weirdly, people loved listening to the cascade of titles so it made the cut and for *Wag!* I resurrected it. I assigned a physical gesture to each book title until I had a vocab I could shape-shift in a few ways that might engage and entertain the viewer if performed in two very different manners. The key was to startle the eye with physical **precision** while speaking the titles in a very **relaxed** voice so as to best associate the movements with the book. This trick of revealing the code for what the viewer is about to see is an aesthetic tool of mine and I have worked with it for some time. It's subtle but I do believe that even unconsciously, if you see movement set in one context, and then the same movement in another context, it's as though you receive a little gift or *cadeau* when you recognize it. In this case when I invited surprise guests to the stage and they performed an economical version of the book list vocab in unison, the audience got a little thrill of recognition, which I hoped added to the pleasure of what they were watching.

I had been attempting to shift the pain of my brother's death with all manner of activities in what I called 'the cheering up program', for many months before deciding to go into the theatre with it. *Wag!* did the job for me of moving from my lonely inner landscape into the theatre of community where everyone has some connection to loss. It is by far the most personal piece I have made and for that reason I performed and toured it only briefly, preferring to let it go once the pain had indeed shifted and I was indeed cheered. I'll finish this sidebar with a quote from the show in which I outline some of the methods I had been employing to find solace:

So I listen to music and freak out dogs. Besides happy young George Gershwin, who is definitely part of the cheering up program, sometimes I listen to less obviously cheerful stuff like Eric Whitacre, the rock star of choral music — a misnomer if ever there was one— but choral music has a rock star and it's him, handsome-like-a-movie star, Eric Whitacre with his long hair and his You Tube cyber choir mega choral hit. It's pretty great. And of course Radiohead is ever present in the playlist. Thom Yorke seems worried and sad sometimes too or at least he used to. Seems a bit more 'DJ' happy lately. Anyways these guys aren't really making 'feel good' music so much as they are making 'feel' music. And that in itself *is* part of the cheering up program, you know, getting into my own heart and head and feeling things full value, which I think helps get you to a place of resolution — it's a term I like better than closure. I am not the closure type. Big, sad life stuff? I don't want to close it. I want to feel it and understand it for awhile and then I just want it to slip away in its own time, diminishing like the chords of a beautiful melancholic song, slow fade to silence ....

Part Two

*The Observer
the Observed
and the Process
of Observation*

Photo: Trudie Lee

Chapter Six

THE THEATRE OF PERCEPTION

Before moving onto the methods for making a performance plan come to life we are going to 'cleanse the palette' and take a trip into the world of perception and aesthetics that make up the practice of Chris Cran.

Chris is a visual artist, a painter with a vast and multi-faceted career spanning forty years and various genres of painting from still life to portraiture to abstraction. His work also includes 'sampling' from Pop art, Photorealism, and Modernist Abstraction, at creative will. He is a successful, highly regarded artist and a beloved and valued mentor to countless young artists, moving about the world of fine art with generosity and humour; in fact his sense of humour sets him apart from the academics and theorists which that rarest world of visual art conjures up.

An immediate and warm presence, Chris is fascinated, curious and happy to share whatever perceptions he may have about the world around him, when discussing what he sees. I had enjoyed a lengthy ongoing dialogue with him, leading to his joining the Lab faculty in 1998, about what he saw when he looked at the stage and in particular when I was on it! This was far more than a series of lovely feedback sessions about my performances because of the formal elements that Chris talked about when observing my work.

Being onstage for most of my life meant that as I had matured towards my adult self, I had learned that one must be careful about not pandering to the audience, not over selling, not working from the ego to make a real connection with them. This humble goal had the unintended consequence of learning to be un-inquisitive about what it was that the viewer saw when I performed. Also, I had joined the ranks of those who simply cannot read reviews, not because of a bad notice but oddly because of a glowing one. I had toughed out some mean reviews by sticking my chin out, standing up a little taller than my almost six feet and deciding that someone calling me 'ubiquitous' and my work, in one case, 'shockingly poor' was simply an opinion that I could take or leave, so I left it. But reading a radiant paragraph about a 'transcendent' moment I had achieved one opening night messed with my **calm organized presence** onstage the following night, when I could barely get through the same monologue for my self-conscious anxiety to rescale the dizzying heights and once again 'transcend'. Yikes.

That was that, and I determined to never again allow a theatre critic's words, good or bad into my playing brain and to instead trust the rehearsal process, the director and my own instincts to guide me. Luckily the entire OYR company, from managers Grant Burns and Stephen Schroeder to the publicists, front of house staff, stage management and my fellow ensemble members understood and honoured my request to 'include me out' of any discussion of reviews.

From that time on I have remained blissfully ignorant of what the media says and reliant only on how the audience reacts and their post-show comments to assess how

Chris Cran artworks installed at the National Gallery of Canada.

the performance is going. Then once I am finished a run, I ask a small handful of trusted colleagues and friends, whose opinions I respect, to share their thoughts. However, this habit of steering clear of feedback had contributed to my blocking any curiosity I might have about being watched on a stage. This is, until Chris began working with OYR.

Blake had invited him to design a few shows for us; my play *Breeder* and a few years later, a devised piece called, *Permission*. It was exhilarating to talk with Chris about the formal elements of composition and how they worked onstage from his perspective as a visual artist. There was a refreshing freedom in the conversation that allowed me to think objectively about how I staged the work and my own playing in the space.

He talked about the **theatre of perception** and **exterior** and **interior framing devices**, comparing and contrasting live theatre with cinema and painting. The relationship between the observer and the observed and the process of observation fascinated him, and I became aware of how constrained and embarrassed I felt to admit that I was curious about being observed even though I was making art that plainly relied upon being seen!

There was a lingering confusion in my mind that to want information about what people saw when I performed could be a hungering for ego gratification, but Chris discussed what he saw in formal terms, which was revelatory and extremely useful. He saw how the light framed the actor and invited the audiences' eye and how the composition of the stage affected the focus. Further to that, he spoke about the relationship of player to the audience and how the player's eyes lifted into the light could reveal so much.

Blake was always requesting the ensemble to play with the eyes lifted and it was so interesting to hear Chris

Two productions that Chris designed, Breeder *(1994) with Mark Bellamy, and* Permission *(1998) with Lindsay Burns. Chris also styled and designed the poster for* Featherland *(2001).*

correlate the simple effectiveness of two small orbs lifting and reflecting light, confirming for me the power I felt in using my eyes and my gaze when I performed.

It's interesting to note that despite the fact that classical dance training is all about how to hold the attention of the viewer with a combination of technique and aesthetics, ballet and modern dancers are usually choreographed very specifically to avoid direct eye contact with the audience. The dancer's focus stays inside the kinesphere even when the eyes are lifted, stopping at the 'membrane' of their personal space and allowing the audience to gaze upon them but not to meet or confront that gaze. It is almost in bad taste to use the face and the eyes for any communication because it detracts from the purity or the abstraction of the movement and introduces personality, which is often antithetical to the choreographer's goals.

Working with One Yellow Rabbit had introduced me to the Brechtian notions of total theatre, which broke the fourth wall to address the audience directly. Michael Green and Blake Brooker were not calling what we did 'Brechtian' or espousing anything other than our own rock 'n roll rules, or lack thereof, which was, for me, the best thing about working with them; nonetheless as I learned more about Brecht and Beckett and especially Jerzy Grotowski, I began to see that there was a lineage that we were engaging with. This brand of intimate performance theatre was bringing me into direct contact with my audience all the time, and yet the conversation with Chris was the first time that I thought about the players' eyes as an element within the greater composition looking out to the audience as much as being looked at. It confirmed the power of the eyes and the relationship between the viewer and the viewed, giving me a new perspective on 'holding focus' (not to be confused with 'stealing focus'), as a formal choice that had nothing to do with ego and functioned as a another communication tool to be understood and used. So I invited Chris to teach at the Lab and to keep this conversation going about 'perception, the observer, and the observed' for the benefit of all the participants.

Framing Devices
Theatre is the seeing place and we rightfully spend much of our energy thinking about what the content is that we are asking people to see. In his practice, Chris found himself thinking not only about the contents of a canvas but also about the edges of what the viewer would see. Looking at the work of early landscape paintings by Nicholas Poussin and Claude Lorrain, he had noted that they favoured an asymmetrical composition, with perhaps a big tree on one side and a small tree on the other creating an interior

framing device that directed attention to a zig zag path in the middle meandering into a distant site of reverie and the illusion of space. He also realized the trees kept the viewers' attention from drifting to the edge of the canvas and beyond, where the illusion would collapse.

Framing became a big consideration in his own forays into space, and he remains deeply interested in what frames his content, which even extends to thinking about the gallery wall on which a painting will hang. The wall provides the context for understanding that this is a finished work and is therefore the first **framing device** or portal that the viewer will come upon that brings them inwards to a field of perception. Once there, the eye moves to the edge of the painting, the actual picture frame. Certain information accompanies that perception, for example; an ornate gilt frame informs the viewer differently than a plain wooden frame does. Knowing that human beings are **meaning making machines,** his work is concerned primarily with engaging the viewer and inviting them to make their own meaning of what they see. How and what they perceive is as much a part of the painting as the work itself. The act of observing invites the viewer into the 'site of reverie' or whatever depth and space he is making with paint on a flat surface.

It is all in the perception and Chris encouraged the Labbits to consider exterior and interior framing devices when making their work. What is the portal? Where does the performance begin? What is the exterior framing device your work is staged within? Once defined, be it a proscenium, a black box, a found indoor space or a meadow, what is the interior framing device that will bring the audience focus to where you want it? What is the 'edge of perception' for the viewing public and how aware of those edges and that relationship are you as a theatre maker and/or player?

In 1998 when Chris began this conversation within the Lab, this idea of experimenting with the framing devices had a correlation with postmodern theatre-making which also questioned where the performance began, but the idea was still a relatively new one. Although postmodern performance had been growing and morphing since the 1980s, most professional theatre-making was still rooted in the traditional practice where it was safe to assume that the play one was attending would not begin until the house lights went down and the action onstage began. Thus, the frame or the 'edge of the performance' was predictably established. Shifting that experience and rethinking where 'the edge of the performance' or where the theatre experience began for the audience was invigorating and gave both the audience and the onstage artists a fresh perspective.

Chris drew a parallel between visual art and theatre, awakening the Lab participants to examples from painting and reinforcing this idea that **everything is watchable**, contained in some kind of frame, and that we observers will immediately try to comprehend and understand what we are seeing. He talked about the evolution of the nervous system and how we have a persistent need to draw conclusions and have certainty about what we see. This is thanks to our earliest evolutionary experiences that taught us we need to know that "there is not a tiger in the bush." We may have lost the fear of tigers for the most part but the alertness still exists and can be directed by the art-maker to entice the viewer to take notice and enter into a specific experience of observation.

He also reminded them that as we stare into our scopic field, what we see is limited and has edges that fade out of focus in our peripheral vision. The landscape painter aims to create an illusion for us, so that in looking at their landscape we remain persuaded that what we are seeing continues beyond the edge of the canvas – that there are other trees and other paths. So in creating some kind of theatrical illusion what are the edges of the theatre? What is the site of reverie? There exists a whole host of questions in common and a shared belief in composition structured to serve both the observer and observed, plus to highlight the idea that performance and painting are both essentially about the process of observation.

Photo: Trudie Lee

THE EROTIC IRONY OF OLD GLORY

"The conquest of the fear of death
is the recovery of life's joy!"
— Joseph Campbell

In 1990, OYR produced a show called *The Erotic Irony of Old Glory* created and performed by Mark Christmann, Neil Cadger and me. The show began as the audience walked into the space. They immediately heard the voice of Joseph Campbell talking about death and dying and saw the three of us clinging to small perches mounted on the rear wall as though lying flat on the floor in a murder scene viewed from above. (Must just add that it was no mean feat doing so; the perches were tiny two-inch ledges and we hung there motionless for the fifteen or twenty minutes it took to get the public seated!)

Right away they understood this would be something a little different; a *noir*-like murder mystery permeated by existential anxiety, which the voiceover seemed to be addressing and soothing. As they took their seats and their eyes adjusted to the low light, the startling effect of looking down on a crime scene was helped by the large patches of gleaming blood, two chairs and a small side table that we hung so that the furniture was standing on the wall next to our bodies. The volume of the lecture slowly faded with the house lights until viewers were sitting in the dark, and in silence. Suddenly we fell off the wall and into the lighted playing space with a vertiginous slam and launched into our wildly physical dance drama about three characters stuck in a 1930s radio play and forced to relive their traumatic love triangle to its murderous conclusion, over and over.

Every element of the production was geared to illuminate the intense urgency of the oversized characters trapped in their *noir* world, floating in the ether on electromagnetic radio waves from which they were desperate to escape. Entering a different universe through the portal of the theatre doors and finding three bodies framed on the back wall perpendicular to the audience view, then suddenly thrown onto the same plane provided three separate framing devices and three separate vantage points for the players to play from, and for the viewers to observe from, setting the world of the play up just as we wished it to be.

Chapter Seven

PUNCTUM AND *STUDIUM*

ROLAND BARTHES, 1915–1980, was a French literary theorist, philosopher, linguist, critic, and semiotician who, after his mother died in 1977, wrote a beautiful book called *Camera Lucida: Reflections on Photography*. Inspired by a childhood photograph of her that had become profoundly meaningful to him in his grief, the book was his attempt to explain why some photographs affect the individual viewer more than others.

Most photos of his mother had an obvious symbolic meaning, but what was it about this particular image of her that held him with such lasting emotion over the many others in his possession? Finally he used two Latin words: *studium* and *punctum* to bring clarity.

When looking at multiple photographs of a similar cultural subject or subjects, Barthes used **studium** to describe a free ranging interest,

> ... a kind of general, enthusiastic commitment, of course but without special acuity. It is by **studium** that I am interested in so many photographs.

He goes on to call **studium** merely "a polite interest," culturally, politically, or aesthetically and that **studium** was a word to describe "the order of liking, not of loving" a series of photographs. For 'loving' he used the Latin word **punctum**, something that broke or punctuated the **studium**, an "element which rises from the scene, shoots out of it like an arrow, and pierces me." It was deeply personal and subjective and only some images would stay with him because of some arrow-like detail that had wounded or 'pierced' him. [1]

Chris Cran introduced Barthes' concepts of **punctum** and **studium** to the Labbits to name the unnamable, the detail in a work of art that affects the viewer in ineffable ways. His contention is that once grasped, this idea – i.e. that only some elements in some works of art leap out and pierce an individual viewer – is a valuable tool for the artist. This is because it alerts them to take note when it happens, to reflect on it in relationship to their own creative impulses, and to ask themselves how it might inform their own individual personal aesthetic.

Chris tells his painting students to study art history and take note when they love something in a historical painting, recording it in what he calls a **journal of aesthetics**, a compendium of favourite aesthetic details to refer to when thinking about one's own work. Of course, it tied in beautifully to the central question of the OYR Lab: 'Who are you now?'

As was made clear in Part 1, the Lab openly invites the Labbits to explore and challenge their own **aesthetic preferences,** which can only happen once those preferences are recognized and named. The **punctum alert** is a tool for discovering and naming that which you love and **punctum** is now a useful part of the One Yellow Rabbit vocabulary; especially when the work reaches the discernment phase and the contributing artists can express a strong feeling they have about something as 'their **punctum**'. The

---

1   References in this paragraph are from the First American Edition of Barthes' *Camera Lucida*, Publisher, Farrar, Straus, and Giroux (1981). Chapter 10/11, pages 26, 27.

Photos: Matt McKinney

The Lab: Heather Ware in her performance piece "Punctums, How to Change Your Life."

ensemble tends to respect and value this potent emotional and/or intuitive response to something that has had a lasting effect on an individual either during a rehearsal period or even outside of OYR activity, in the work of others.

The Lab has appropriated the word to the extent that at the end of each day, we laze about in the theatre seats and exchange **punctums**. Sometimes, the Labbits speak of something outside the theatre walls that struck them at lunch or enroute to the space, but it more often relates directly to the experiences they have throughout the day creating and sharing.

This exercise of sharing **punctums** has been an excellent way to assess the effectiveness of the methods and tools being put forward over the last twenty years by the faculty to the participants. Not everyone has a **punctum** every day, which is fine, but if they do, they tend to talk about it with a sense of poignancy and emotional investment that has been tremendously important for us all – Blake, Chris, and me – to hear. We are, after all, genuinely curious to know what touches the artists about what we are suggesting each day in our sessions, and this form of feedback, good or bad, seems honest and heart-felt as opposed to analytical or judgmental.

But beyond that, the term gives artistic agency to the person who has been pierced or wounded or moved by something. One needn't justify or explain a **punctum**, it may just be some tingle in the nervous system, some pleasure or pain that thrills and shifts perspective. It may result in tears or delighted laughter, a shocked silence or a reverent lift in the spirit – and it's yours! You felt it. Even if by chance someone else agrees with you, it is still yours and that gives you intelligence about who you are aesthetically, which is the realm of understanding for the artist. As Chris Cran says, there is no one like you. You must privilege that and see where it takes you or you submit to an authority outside of yourself. We, who appreciate art and artists, are interested only in the authority you find to express yourself.

Fetishes

Fetish is a loaded word and most often elicits the sexual connotation as used in psychoanalysis. But somehow the Lab conversation about punctums invited a discussion of how a strong reaction to an idea or object could become something to which the artist might grow fetishistically attached and play an ongoing role in making their art. Did it follow that a punctum could become a non-sexual fetish? Something recognized becomes so powerful that it stays with you until the object or the idea has talismanic resonance and represents a magical power or fascination that can be returned to over and over as an animating force.

OYR most definitely has a tender animal fetish, obvious

in the creation of several plays: *Changing Bodies, The Land, The Animals, Featherland, Fabulous Disaster,* and in our colleague Karen Hines' play *All The Little Animals I've Eaten*, which premiered at OYR. From the very beginning, we Rabbits shared a strong attachment to human/animal relationships, as is obvious even from the name of the company.

The story of the name, One Yellow Rabbit, is a good example of how a fetish for a talismanic object can give name to an enterprise and imbue the participants with a kind of secret power. When Michael and Blake were first setting out to make things happen in the early eighties, they attended a workshop to learn more about fund raising. The person at the registration table insisted they needed an organizational name and Blake wrote down a mysterious combination of number, colour, and animal: One Yellow Rabbit.

When pressed for the meaning he just shrugged. In fact, in a bureau drawer at home, wrapped in an old pillowslip was a small well-loved, raggedy yellow bunny with one eye and a torn ear that had been his childhood companion and had accompanied him on many adventures into his imagination. We all felt the tender magical power that it represented for Blake, the fetish-like attachment to the bunny set free his imagination and seemed to do the same for the rest of the ensemble.

Chris is slightly uncomfortable with the idea of fetish, but admits to having a fetish for paying attention to some formal properties in visual art: space, the sharpness of an edge in contrast with an out-of-focus or misregistered focal point, and interior framing devices that combat the so-called 'tyranny of the rectangle'. To have been present at his career retrospective at the National Gallery of Canada in 2016 was to wander through five galleries full of art. Viewers were made utterly complicit in that they were invited to make their own meaning, an idea that fascinates Chris – another driving force that could fit into this notion of fetish.

There is also an actual object from Chris' childhood that he slowly understood to have fetishistic or talismanic properties, discovered after turning over his creative decision-making to his painting hand. One day several years ago he had found himself wondering if his hand had its own intelligence and picking up the brush, just began to paint whatever his hand wanted, which turned out to be a slightly lopsided, almost cartoon-like interior frame a few inches inside the rectangle of the canvas. His hand just kept repeating the gesture over and over with tremendous pleasure and led to a whole series based on this curvy form that was almost rectangular but soft in opposition to the sharpness of the actual rectangular stretcher.

Ten years later, he was remembering a painting that his great grandfather had brought over from England, signed 'A.E. Chaton, Portrait Painter to Her Majesty the Queen 1830', which had hung in the family home while he grew up; a portrait of a lady framed in an ornate gilded frame, slightly asymmetrical with rounded corners. Suddenly he realized that the frame was the basic shape his hand had abstracted in the gestural painting series of a decade earlier. He retrieved it on the next trip back to Salmon Arm, BC, where he had lived as a child, and brought it back to his studio. He had a 3D scan made of the frame and reproduced it in three sizes. His attraction to this frame and the form itself has fueled him unconsciously and consciously in a fetish-like manner and wound up contributing significantly to his body of work.

His suspicion of the idea of fetish as an animating force arose when he found himself fetishistically attached to searching for space to emerge in his paintings until, as he says "the search itself was the fetish, becoming more important than what was being searched for and taking on the mechanics of greed." However in asking the Lab participants to consider whether or not they had any talismanic objects or practices, he agreed that as a tool it might, once again, point them in the direction of identifying personal creative traits to inspire, augment and bring an animating power to their work.

Blake Brooker also speaks about his intense curiosity as a fetish for information gathering, something that drives all of his creativity. One need only have a conversation with him and/or read his plays, to understand what he means, for it most certainly is a fetish-like attention, fascination and appetite for the unexpected details in the lives and situations of others. This often results in an idiosyncratic poetic style that is at the same time emotionally and intellectually viable and inviting.

The art-making life is one of trial and error and articulating your own drives and fascinations will put an advantageous tool to work discovering what might be unique and distinctive about your perspective.

Activity PLAY
*Just this: Keep a **journal of aesthetics** for yourself. When you experience theatre or film, hear music, look at visual art or just wander in the world observing and being observed, talking to and listening to other people, smelling the air and feeling your surroundings, be attentive to what attracts your general interest (identify **studium**) and if something should 'rise from the scene, shooting out of it like an arrow, and pierce you', write it down in that journal. Think about your **aesthetic preferences** in relationship to those **punctums**. Be alert and awake to whatever you might name a **fetish** if you begin to see a trend or a pattern and let it galvanize you to aesthetic investigation.*

ALIEN BAIT

"These stories, whether they're real or imagined,
are interesting stories anyway!"
— Blake Brooker

There is no doubt that Blake Brooker's sharing of his childhood totemic fetish, his one-eyed yellow bunny that gave us our name, played a big part, along with the alchemy of the people and their skills and aesthetics, in giving OYR a sense of destiny and purpose. We have been and remain forever charged by the notion of uncensored, imaginative play with one another and all manner of fetish like interests can be held accountable for various pieces in our body of work. One that stands out was the result of Michael Green's utter attachment to the book, *Communion: A True Story* by Whitley Strieber, a terrifying and thrilling book about alien encounters. He talked about it incessantly and was so driven by the feelings it elicited in him that he became an amateur 'UFOlogist', attending conferences and collecting as much data about the various phenomena surrounding UFOs as possible. For years, the rest of the company had humoured him, teasing him about his dressing room staple reading; *The Fortean Times* magazine, a quarterly publication of the genuinely weird and supernatural, and about his fetish for aliens. But eventually the seriousness with which he conducted his research began to impress us, so much so that we made an eerie investigation in a show called *Alien Bait*. The show was organized around two principles: 'Experts' and 'Abductees' coming together to reveal and challenge the information that surrounded the phenomenon. I distinctly remember battling a desire to severely judge the concept, thanks to my own ignorance and bias against the topic. In retrospect, there was a healthy dose of fear too; I had begun reading *Communion* and almost immediately put it down because of how frightening it was. But also I was worried that the campy nature of the general culture surrounding the whole thing would detract from a serious theatrical investigation. How wrong I was.

Michael arrived on day one of rehearsal with books, stacks of paper, reports, first-person accounts and transcripts of hypnotic regressions of abductees. The concept got real for me, and I think for all of us, when we realized that it didn't matter whether or not one believed in alien abduction, there were many people lost in a maze of fear, confusion, and sorrow because they believed they had been taken. The experience made them the loneliest people alive.

The stories were powerful, scary, detailed and deeply, deeply moving. We divided the scenes between abductees arriving and speaking at a UFOlogy conference and experts and skeptics gathered in panels to give evidence, or debunk. Although this was just before the internet came into wide spread use, Michael had amassed an extraordinary body of literature, taped testimony and video to pull from, and we became more and more respectful of the responsibility we had to these sufferers and to those researchers who dedicated their lives to helping them. Inspired by what we learned from reading and listening to these people, we made improvisational studies with Blake leading the members of the ensemble into *faux* hypnotic regressions to recall the details of their abduction. Although we were improvising in the safety of a rehearsal room, we were shaken by the poignancy and loneliness we experienced by embodying their plights. The premiere production was so frightening that we realized if we were to tour it and not leave people with nightmares, we had to balance the terror with comic relief, which we loaded into the roles of the experts who were also based on real people, many of whom we felt could stand to take a ribbing. The show played to skeptics, believers, and the firmly undecided and was a breakthrough for the company. *Alien Bait* introduced the style of investigative inquiry that we employed in other shows like *Somalia Yellow* and *The History of Wild Theatre*.

Chapter Eight

SILENCE, EXILE, AND CUNNING

W E WILL TAKE A DETOUR from the discussion of Chris Cran's research and areas of interest to talk about another essential person in the extended OYR ensemble and his contribution to the Lab. A close colleague for much of the last twenty-five years, the amazing polymath and playwright, John Murrell has been one of those incredibly generous people who immediately opened his heart and mind to the upstart Rabbits in the early nineties. John made available his remarkable experience and knowledge and became part of our creative family, writing three plays for the ensemble: *Death in New Orleans, Taking Shakespeare,* and *Fat Jack Falstaff's Last Hour;* joining the company to perform the latter two. John is intimate with much of OYR's body of work and has long been intrigued by the methods and methodologies for making theatre art that are kindred to, but occasionally in direct contrast, to his own. He even went so far as joining us in a creation process for a piece called *Damien Frost,* which, at this writing, is scheduled to premiere January 2019 at the High Performance Rodeo.

As a member of the initial Lab faculty from 1997 to 2002, John took up a hammer and chiselled away with us to find a common working vocabulary, much of which endured and which you have been reading as **bolded text** in these pages. He was specifically interested in our triadic mantra of **Precision, Economy, and Relaxation** and could appreciate how these principles translated to the stage in what he called the 'broadcasting' of the creative content. However, these principles were in opposition to what he felt was, and still is, necessary for him as a playwright: a process of entering **'the cave'** and setting himself up as a 'receiver' tuning into whatever signals the universe might have to offer him about his chosen theme.

For John, the bustling hub of the performance creation room was the destination where the broadcasting would begin, but only after his retreat into the cave, where he could cultivate **Silence, Exile, and Cunning**, his own triadic formula borrowed from James Joyce's classic modernist novel, *A Portrait of the Artist as a Young Man*. Joyce's words are memorable indeed and bear quoting in any discussion of artistic identity:

> I will tell you what I will do and what I will not do. I will not serve that in which I no longer believe, whether it calls itself my home, my fatherland, or my church: and I will try to express myself in some mode of life or art as freely as I can and as wholly as I can, using for my defence the only arms I allow myself to use — silence, exile and cunning.

In the Lab setting, John was exuberant and had marvelous suggestions for what to take on the journey into the cave to stimulate and augment what it was that could be received by the artist poised to write. He brought in a box of treasures: essential oils, a smooth glass object, a velvet scarf, an orange, and a small Zuni fetish of a horny toad – a

*The Lab: Guest Instructor John Murrell. reciting from Falstaff.
Bringing forward iterations of the deeply personal.*

creature he called his spirit animal; tough and bony back with a soft underbelly which, if stroked, relaxed the little lizard into an ecstatic open stretch, all of which John feels perfectly describes his own nature. His treasure box also contained many more tactile and sensuous things to feel and smell and taste, all aimed at stimulating the senses as he charged the Labbits to go deep into their own caves.

He would ask for silence and have them close their eyes as he placed one thing in front of each person to decipher. It was a master class in opening the self to the world of receptivity and the artists were often moved to tears as they took up their pens and began scribbling. They responded beautifully to the metaphor of the cave and to the notions of **silence** and **exile**, which were more understandable tools than **cunning** proved to be.

As discussions progressed, it was clear that the Labbits wondered at how Joyce and John implemented the word 'cunning' that suggested shrewdness and deceit. To understand James Joyce is a study of what drove him to self-exile from Ireland, the times and the context in which he lived and wrote. John simply believes that there is an element of cunning necessary to make a life as a writer, and urged the group to be ruthlessly focused when it came to carving out their own place and finding their individual voices, something he had done for himself. Because he is also one of the kindest and most thoughtful people alive, this exhortation seemed less about sly calculation and conniving and more about artful self-determination.

What followed from these sessions was to be a very big part of the development of the Lab, along with the use of the cut-up, which we will come back to shortly. Chris, Blake, John and I always followed up the three weeks of the Lab to talk about what we had learned and what seemed useful or not for the artists. We would naturally discuss the ten-minute offerings that each artist presents on the final two days. Although Blake gave each person a poetic suggestion that they were free to use however they wished, there was no rule, no limit except the ten-minute length and the use of the available lights in the grid, which they'd grown familiar with over the three weeks.

During John's tenure, we became aware that there was a strong tendency for confessional work, brought to the stage in varying iterations of the deeply personal. John was curious about how forays into the cave influenced that outcome. Frankly, we all worried that occasionally the artists were overly exposing themselves, and us, to what was better meant for a private diary or journal. However in designing the Lab I had been quite clear that there would be no public feedback about the final pieces, so we kept our thoughts to ourselves, unless specifically asked by the performer.

I did not want to conclude the experience of examining

one's own creative identity with a pronouncement of yea or nay, and was far more interested in providing these Labbits with a jumping-off point to find out for themselves how their aesthetics registered with a public. This was not a school and we were not arbiters to give a grade. Instead this was a place where for a three-week period, you could be yourself, work hard at serious play, and do whatever you wanted for ten minutes without judgment or critical reception from anyone.

Beyond the time spent at the Big Secret Theatre, many of those ten-minute pieces have gone on to expanded lives and full theatrical runs, exposing the artist to the thumbs up and/or down of the actual marketplace, leading them to discern for themselves about how to proceed. John's concern had to do with the egalitarian empowerment of each and every person to leave the Lab without any sense of what we felt the chances for success were out there in the 'real world'. Did we not owe it to them to give an honest assessment of what they did? My intuition said no, that the Lab was its own experience and that it was not our business to define success or failure in any way and that the individual must decide or discover for themselves.

My colleagues respected that decision but we continued to grapple with the confessional, and whether or not there was some connection to the emotional sensory place they found in John's cave. At any rate we weren't lucky enough to continue the research with him after he was appointed the head of theatre at the Banff Centre, which fully occupied him from 2000 through 2010. Although he is no longer able to be a full faculty member, he still visits as *éminence grise* and dazzles the group for an afternoon with his soulful questions and his uncanny ability to inspire and move people to both laughter and tears.

Chapter Nine

THE BURROUGHS EFFECT AND CUT-UPS

Speaking of fetishes, all of One Yellow Rabbit, but especially Blake Brooker, Chris Cran, and John Murrell, have long been fans of the Beat poets, especially the granddaddio, William S. Burroughs. Burroughs was a brilliant and innovative writer, an intellectual outlier of the times, troubled by his homosexuality as a young man, somewhat misogynistic, hilarious, addicted to heroin and tremendously influential to the counter culture, especially to rock stars who read him and cultivated relationships with him until his death in 1997. He was an absolutely challenging and yet inspiring artist because of his fearless skewering of the powerful controlling entities that drove the dominant culture.

Burroughs' work, written in his inimitable poker-face style, often achieved quite breathtaking feats of technical and poetic expertise, while being hugely entertaining. In the early 1980s, he took his show on the road and gave readings sitting at a desk with nothing but a microphone and his distinctive gravel voice. When friends brought him to Calgary in 1986, I remember being amazed as this grandfatherly man shambled out onto stage and proceeded to hold the mostly very young, punk-filled audience in thrall like no grampa any of us had ever known. Burroughs' famous routines, likened to depraved vaudeville acts, had been recorded at one of these sold-out readings and were collectors' items then and now. They are dark and bizarre but genuinely hilarious. Chris credited the recordings with getting him through a personal slump by providing him with endless entertainment, intellectual solace, and laughter.

In 1961, Burroughs wrote an experimental trilogy of novels called *The Nova Trilogy* employing the **cut-up technique.** In the late 1950s, he was introduced to the cut-up while staying in Paris at the 'Beat Hotel' with his great friend, the visual artist Brion Gysin. Gysin was cutting the edges of a mount for a piece of art using a Stanley blade on top of a stack of newspapers. When he lifted it, he discovered he had cut up the text of the papers below into random sequences and showed Burroughs who was dazzled and took the results seriously. Seizing on the concept as a strategy, he began to experiment with his own writing, cutting and reassembling and eventually incorporating these word collages in his work. The method is well-loved and used by many visual artists and musicians and poets like David Bowie, Patti Smith, and Thom Yorke, only three of many who famously use the cut-up to construct the music, poetry, and lyrics of their songs.

Please Observe the Following Performance

Chris introduced the **cut-up** into his Lab sessions as a way of responding to the mini-performances by various guests that he presents during the last session of each day. To add to the delight and mystery of the experience, the guest is kept a secret. Chris asks the Labbits to take their seats, the house lights come down and an onstage special comes up. Using the fine art of repetition, Chris amuses his audience, always introducing some slight change in his delivery as he emerges from backstage into the light and announces:

The Lab: Chris Cran working with the Labbits on the cut-up technique of idea development, pioneered by William Burroughs.

"Please observe the following performance."

Over the years, one after another of the amazing colleagues we consider part of the extended OYR ensemble have generously contributed a brief performance, normally around ten minutes, which incidentally is the length of the final presentation we ask the Labbits themselves to create and perform. Our intention with these mini performances has been to offer a small gift, a *cadeau* that asks the participants of the Lab to observe, respond, and feed back the experience in a circular relationship with **the observer** and **the observed** in a **process of observation**.

They find themselves sitting in the dark with no idea of what the day's performance will bring, and although they're tired by late afternoon, they become alert and focused when the guests, performers at the top of their game, present **undeniable** work that makes clear the triad of **Precision, Economy, and Relaxation**. A brief list of some of those who have honoured us with their work includes Andy Curtis, Michael Green, Karen Hines, Davida Monk, Bruce McCulloch, Chris Hunt, Kris Demeanor, John Murrell, Bobby Wiseman, Jakob Koranyi, Peter Hinton and the entire cast of *Radioheaded 2,* to name but a few.

There is always a wonderful sense of expectation and it's not uncommon for our guest stars to feel a little rush of nerves themselves before stepping out on the Big Secret stage, knowing there are curious and discerning eyes on them. Once they finish, the onstage lights go down, the houselights come back up, and we leave the Labbits in silence to record their observations and write non-stop for five minutes. They are not trying to 'write well', only to get something on the page that is an immediate and honest response to what they have just seen – double-spaced on one side only. Once the five minutes is up, they sit on the stage with scissors and glue-sticks and the cutting begins; every line cut and divided in half until they have a small pile of phrases to draw from, in random order, to paste back onto a fresh page.

As the days go by, it becomes apparent that some artists prefer to 'curate' the manner in which they are cutting and/or pasting, while some stick to the randomness of the chance operation. It doesn't matter, as long as they stay true to the playful nature of the exercise and get a new artifact made quickly. Once the **cut-up** is complete, they sit for a few minutes and read over what they have assembled, accompanied by the odd laugh, gasp, groan, or a thoughtful 'hmmmmm' as they do so. Then they're back in their seats with the guest performer seated in the middle of the front row, and one by one, come onstage into the same light to read their cut-up.

The Lab: Scissors, glue stick, and small piles of phrases that formulate the cut-ups.

There is a fair bit of nonsensical language but it's punctuated by strangely effective poetics or obviously wonderful turns of phrase that delight and surprise. As time progresses, the gang become more confident in their readings, ranging from neutral to more obviously theatrical takes. Thanks to the non-judgment rule, they make bold choices and become increasingly inured to the fear of failure, resulting in regular flashes of brilliance.

There is plenty of laughter and sudden emotional resonance and the readings are often entertaining and moving. The general tone of the original observation shimmers through, but the **cut-ups** are something unto themselves. They tend to elevate the language of response away from personal like or dislike, revealing more about the speaker than about their subject. We don't applaud but there is some appropriate beatnik finger snapping at a particularly strong line or well-played bit. Most importantly, the circular relationship of observation, response, re-crafting and feed-back provides the artists with repeated opportunities to observe and be observed in a non-judgmental working space.

The secondary benefit is without doubt the realization that they have not written something so much as the cut-up has. After the first day, Chris suggests they 'flash edit' by striking out words or phrases of their work to seek out poetic gems or sentences that lift the language and pierce the air with accidental moments of genius. Chris always cites his punctum, never forgotten, which the late Bill Torre delivered back one day many years ago to a chorus of finger snaps: "She moved forward like a red carpet."

The artists are encouraged to record their punctums as they listen to their onstage colleagues and hopefully it occurs that fantastic language can be 'found' as well as written. Language that might open an exhilarating door to one's **playful** self and once again, relieves the burden of having to 'write well'. There are no firm rules. The **cut-up** can be used as a warm-up, it can offer up a line that might initiate or ornament a full monologue or it can lend itself to becoming a performance piece. It can be played with and rearranged into something new, or left on the drawing board as an amusing exercise. Regardless, it has a place in the tool kit waiting to be put to work.

There was one other curious correlation with the introduction of the cut-up into the Lab working vocabulary. Referring back to chapter eight and the work John Murrell introduced when he took the Labbits 'into **the cave**', which freed them to find and record their personal truths, but also led to the over-exposed territory of the **confessional** in some of the final projects.

Being the utterly brilliant wordsmith that he is, John's entering into the depths of the cave has given us plays full of emotional power, wit, and daring that speak to his great knowledge of human experience as translated through the mastery of his craft. When he enters that sensory world of **silence, exile, and cunning,** and accesses what is truly beautiful, painful, and funny to him, he also brings to bear an exceptional body of experience and skill to light his writing table and guide his pen. The Labbits also discovered their truths but perhaps only those with their own body of work behind them were able to similarly translate the feelings to the page and the stage with no danger of sentiment or embarrassment.

The first summer John was no longer able to join us just so happened to coincide with Chris' introduction of the cut-up and we couldn't help but notice a decided change in the final performances. We wondered if the revelatory nature of taking first 'splash' emotional response and manipulating it to express an experience was having an effect on how the artists approached their pieces.

We were in no way certain of the correlation and in fact, outside of long conversations about it, have no evidence except that we saw less raw pain and drama and a more pronounced aesthetic development along with more playfulness emerge. It also occurred to us that possibly we were becoming more adept at sharing the information and layering the experience of the Lab so as to better serve the artists and more effectively enable them to use the tools we laid out. But there was no doubt that the penchant for work that veered towards therapy or journal art seemed to fall away.

It could also have been a shift in the general theatre practice of the times, which resulted in a lot more devised performance theatre and therefore higher expectations that although the work might include a confessional element, it should at the same time bring strong theatrical aesthetic principles to bear and elevate the material from the raw state. Our close colleague David van Belle, put it this way, quoting performance theorist Richard Schechner: "Life is raw. Art is cooked."

Activity PLAY

Find something that is of interest to you, a performance, a piece of music, an art book or an overheard coffee shop conversation. Observe it for however long you wish. Then set your timer to five minutes and keeping your pen on the page, double-spaced, one side only, splash out a written record of your observation.

Stop writing after five minutes and get out your kindergarten craft kit, scissors, and glue and go to work cutting up the text line by line. Then cut those lines in half, keeping full words intact. Toss. Pick up a random phrase and glue it down, continuing until you have reordered everything. Read it aloud a few times. Punctuate it. Flash edit by striking out words or phrases. Look for the gems, **punctums** *or the accidental poetics that have grace and seem to 'work'.*

Or, find an extant text, something you're working on or a famous speech from a favourite play, poem or novel. Copy it. Cut it up. Toss and glue down a new order. Same thing. Read. Punctuate. Edit. Does anything pierce you? Do you find your internal gadget clicking into place with pleasure or intuitive delight?

You may find a gem, a **punctum** *that inspires a new speech, a new paragraph or poem. Follow that impulse and use the cut-up to whatever end. Be alert to how the language may somehow work in new and inventive ways and help you play against preferences.*

Photo: Blake Brooker

THE DREAM MACHINE

"Love? What is it?
Most natural painkiller what there is. Love."
— William S. Burroughs

In 2002, finding themselves at sea in the zeitgeist of 911 and the horror it unleashed, Blake Brooker wrote the lyrics and David Rhymer composed the music of *The Dream Machine*, a hallucinogenic oratorio of songs and poems inspired by the iconoclastic Beat generation and its writers. It was a step forward in the theatrical musical for the company. The piece was unconcerned with narrative or story and was structured around artists who lived way outside the mass culture and the advertising juggernaut that defined those mad men years — artists who pushed into realms of free expression and experimentation.

The Dream Machine itself, a stroboscopic device, was one of those experiments, researched and created in the early 1960s by Brion Gysin with Ian Sommerville and William Burroughs. Two things spurred these "dream mechanics" into the invention. They were aware of chemist and LSD inventor, Dr. Albert Hoffman's research into the effect of hallucinogenic substances on the brain and especially the sense of expanded universal consciousness that resulted; and of Aldous

Huxley's mescaline-inspired book, *Heaven and Hell* (1956), which posited that flickering light could "enrich and intensify" the "visionary experience" induced by psychedelic drugs. Two years later in 1958, Gysin experienced a hallucinatory state while travelling on a bus in France. Canadian writer John Geiger describes the experience in his book *Chapel of Extreme Experience*:

> As the bus passed through a long avenue of trees Gysin, closing his eyes against the setting sun, encountered 'a transcendental storm of color visions.' ... The phenomenon ended abruptly as the bus left the trees. 'Was that a vision? What happened to me?' asked Gysin.

He shared the experience with Burroughs who was tremendously excited by any portal to enlightenment, and then set about developing a machine to

> ... harness the visionary potential of flicker, a device that would make illusory experience available at the flick of a switch: a Dream Machine.

Besides Blake and David *The Dream Machine* ensemble included percussionist Peter Moller and violinist Jonathon Lewis, performers Andy Curtis, Onalea Gilbertson, Michael Green, Brad Payne or alternatively David van Belle, myself, and Chris Cran who designed the show. Being a fellow Beat geek, Chris had the plans for building a Dream Machine which Gysin published in 1986 in a small pamphlet called, *Dreamachine Plans,* published by OV Press, in Denver. He enlisted his then-studio assistant, Scott Christian to do the build and following Gysin's instructions, Scott constructed a three-foot column with cutout rectangles and a light bulb hanging inside, balanced on a turntable that spun at either 45 or 78 rpm.

Once complete, the finished machine was wheeled into the rehearsal room and we all immediately tried it out. We were not stoned on drugs and had varying results but regardless, the machine was now part of the cast and stood majestically centre-stage, inspiring us every time we began our tripped-out oratorio. The machine was impressively lit and had a strong totemic energy as Michael began Allen Ginsberg's powerful poem *America*, an indictment of all that 1950s America had come to be. The ensemble entered, taking one slow-motion step at a time, offsetting the urgent quixotic text with bizarre calm until we reached our places. Ginsberg's last line hung in the air, "America, I'm putting my queer shoulder to the wheel" and the glorious music swirled in.

Although Blake's writing occasionally brought one of the beat artists to life, the

---

Quotes above: John Geiger. *Chapel of Extreme Experience: A Short History of Stroboscopic Light and the Dream Machine.* NY: Soft Skull, 1997.

Photo: Blake Brooker

With Jonathan Lewis, Onalea Gilbertson in The Dream Machine.

piece was far removed from a bio-play and preferred to invoke the magical, hallucinatory and wildly inspired world that the beat denizens occupied; the life of any writer or artist, alone and lonely, or exhilarated in the company of others, but determined to find authentic selfhood.

The songs were intercut with poetics, movement and instrumental forays with Peter and Jonathon joining the actors as we staggered into a deadly game of William Tell or, blasted with white light and searing electric string hooks, launched into choreographed madness. One of the quietest moments in the show was a poignant spoken word piece called "Pain Killer." Sandwiched between a paranoid song of a man lost and stoned in his shabby hotel room trying to write – "Hieroglyphics," and a sad but determined female voice intent on leaving her husband and her shiny chrome kitchen – "Surrounded by Chrome" (favourite lyrics in the show: "The living room is killing me; the bedroom suite is sour"), "Pain Killer" employed repetition, collage and the cut-up. It was based on the last words William Burroughs ever wrote:

"Love? What is it?
Most natural painkiller what there is.
LOVE."

Blake added and changed a few words then let them toss themselves into random sequences that he played with until they served his needs.

"Pain Killer" was my poem to perform and it offered me a challenge with its repetitious, pared down and painful questions about the vagaries of love but it became weirdly effective, tender and sometimes funny once I directly addressed the audience as though the questions had come from them. "Pain Killer" is included twice on the next pages, as written and then with the punctuation used to perform it. These serve as an example of applying the cut-up and collage methods to performative material.

The Dream Machine remains an ensemble favourite for many reasons not the least of which is that it will forever somehow immortalize our dear late brother Michael Green. He ended the play as he began it, holding the audience in thrall, standing alone centre stage, with eyes closed, four inches from the now spinning, flickering device while the rest of us backed slowing away singing: "They dreamed of him, he dreamed of us, she dreamed the dream, I dreamed of you, you dreamed of me, we dreamed of them, they dreamed of him."

Pain Killer

To	Is what want pain
To want	To want is
To want is	Is love pain
To want is to love	To what love is pain
What	To want love is what
To want what	Pain is what
Is to love	Want to love
What love is to want	Love what
What is	Pain is what love is
To what is want	To want
Is love what is	Love is what pain is
To want	Love is the best pain killer
Is want to love	What
What want is to love	Love is the best pain
To want love to what	What love is pain
Want to love is	Is love want
Pain	What
Is pain what to want	Killer love is want
Want pain is to	To want killer love is pain
What is pain	What
Pain is what	Love is the best
Want to pain	Pain killer that can be got

Michael Green. 1957–2015

Punctuated Pain Killer

To…
To want…
To want is…
To want is to love.
What?
To want what is to love?

What love is: to want what is.

To what is want? Is love what is to want?
Is want to love what want is? To love? To want love? To what? Want to love?

Is pain…is pain what to want? Want pain? Is to?…
What is pain?
Pain is what?
'Want pain' is what? 'Want pain' to want?

Is…is love pain?
What?
Love is pain? To want love is what pain is?
What?

Want to love.
Love what?

Pain is what love is.
To want love is what pain is.
Love is the best pain killer.
What?

Love is the best pain. What love is pain?
Is love want?
What?
Killer love is want.
To want killer love is pain
What?
Love is the best pain killer that can be got.

Photo: Richard McDowell

The Big Secret Book insists on using methods that take the place of that fickle thing called inspiration, relying instead on strategies to insure forward momentum. In Part One we focused on the player and their practice, which will sustain and lend strength to the artist's vision. Part Two is concerned with the observer, the observed and the process of observation.

In Part Three, we examine the building of the work itself and take a close look at Blake Brooker's methods and tools: how he sets up a room, how he dives into and develops a concept and especially how he uses limitations to drive the process of generating performative material – all essentials of the OYR house style.

Part Three

Setting up the Room and Making a Performance Plan

Photo: Trudie Lee

Photo: Trudie Lee

Chapter Ten

WHO DOES WHAT?

An idea has you excited, agitated and anxious to begin. The transformation of ideas to playable actions, story development and the creation of a **performance plan** or script is the next big undertaking but just before you leap in, consider first: **who does what** in this process?

It might be construed that **performance theatre** messes with traditionally exclusive roles: Writer. Director. Actor. Choreographer. Composer. Stage Manager. These roles may overlap and layer with everyone generating and contributing text, movement vocabs, or song ideas, but it is probably worth mentioning that some degree of hierarchy will still serve you.

Nothing wrecks the soup quicker than too many chefs. Harken back for a moment to the **preference** studies of Part One and recall the discussion of a room where the dominant energy was **directional** with a tendency for bumpercar-like personality collisions. Nobody wants to break the spirit of a bunch of thoroughbred artists champing at the bit, but a leader can help harness the energy and creativity and guide it towards fruition.

Perhaps you intend to create a solo work, but even then, many soloists feel more confident with a director to act as a performance dramaturge or an outside eye on the work. It would behoove you to be certain that your initial conversation with that director includes a clear discussion of what you, as the 'igniting' artist, needs. For example:

A. "I am making a solo show for myself. I've written it and I know how I want to stage it. Would you consider being my outside eye to help me get it right?"
Is different from—
B. "I wrote a solo show for myself. Will you direct it?

The professional director will hear the difference immediately or they should. 'A' suggests that you wish to self-direct and stage but that you trust them to advise and give notes and suggestions. You are asking for a specific investment from them, while letting them know that you will take creative control, a courtesy which could potentially save both of you from feeling insulted or overwhelmed, but if, as 'B' suggests, you ask them simply to direct your show, remember that they are bringing their skill set to your party, including how they run a room, what they prioritize, and of course their dramaturgical aesthetic preferences. If that is exactly what you want then great, but don't handicap them or yourself if it is not. If it lies somewhere in between, tell them that. Discuss terms so it's understood what you are asking them to do.

If you are the igniting artist and you need a posse to bring your idea to life, think carefully about what you want the working relationships to be. Consider these next two invitations:

A. "I have an idea for a show that I want to develop, direct and perform with a few other artists. I think you'd be perfect for one of the roles if you'd like to work with me."
Is different from—
B. "Do you want to make a show with me?"

'A' clearly lets the other person hear that you have an idea and a plan, and that you wish to lead the project. It's respectful and opens the conversation honestly in a way that allows them to make their decision with eyes wide open. But if you are attracted to another artist or artists and you are curious to start from scratch with no aesthetic agenda except to see what the results of collaboration might be, then 'B' is a fair invitation. It suggests that everything is on the table and introduces the notion of **letting the best idea win**, no matter whose it is. It's a bit more rock and roll; the motivating concept revolves around the persons and their aesthetics and determines the direction of the work, but you might still want to agree on the ground rules and **values** to live and play by.

Of course, there are as many permutations and combinations of ways to collaborate as there are people who want to make theatre. This serves only as a suggestion to consider before you invite or accept an invitation to make new work. (See Sidebar *Who Does What* on pages 132-133)

Values

The mission of the Lab has always been to crack open our tool kits and reveal all to the artists who make their way to The Big Secret Theatre. When we started making theatre in the 1980s, there was a prevalent culture of closed-door exclusivity that made the gleaning of theatrical knowledge from established companies seem nigh impossible, especially for a gang of upstarts like the Rabbits. Of course there were always exceptions to the rule and it was that kind of generosity that influenced the style of mentorship and guidance that the Lab was founded on and that OYR continues to espouse. It has always been central to our ethos to share all the information, knowledge, and methods that have proven useful and effective for us. In approaching the

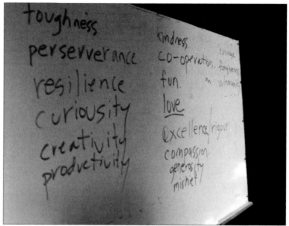

The Lab: Blake Brooker's whiteboard, calling for mantras and visions. Defined here are values decided upon by the group.

creation of this book, someone asked: "Aren't you worried that by writing it all down you are giving away the intellectual capital that is the chief asset and commodity of the OYR artists?" Better to firstly address that question with a discussion of **generosity** and **values**.

Blake always begins his rehearsals and his teaching with the whiteboard in place, a coloured pen in hand, and a call for values to be decided upon by the group. It goes beyond a 'feel good' exercise to kick things off with a nice vibe. Its greater use is as a practical tool if difficulties arise. In that unwelcome circumstance, it is much easier to have tough conversations if everyone present has an agreed-upon set of **values** that work as a lens to examine the problem through. Let's say the ensemble have gathered and agreed that the atmosphere they'd like to work in will include:

1. Creativity without judgment
2. Honesty without harm
3. Curiosity most welcome

4. Perseverance through hardship
5. Productivity balanced with good vibes
6. Cooperation
7. Respect
8. Excellence
9. Generosity and/or best idea wins
10. Discernment when it's time.

These are fairly obvious **values** that folks would probably say are the given when a rehearsal period begins – it could even be said that to discuss values is slightly infantilizing and schoolmarm-ish. The punk rocker of the past would likely snort their derision at such an exercise and even today, there are those who might roll their eyes and insist that adult artists have their own notions of professional decorum and etiquette and to ask for suggestions and write them down is an embarrassing waste of time. Yet strangely many a professional workplace is still vulnerable to unpleasantness and damaging experiences that no one feels equipped to redress. The contention is that this simple conversation is a tool for when the work does *not* go well and most certainly can't hurt when it does. Everyone in the room has an opportunity to make suggestions and in doing so, a contract of agency and accountability is struck.

But beware; too much sensitivity is as bad as none and to be on the defensive hunt for 'wrong doing' could also destroy the quest to make good art and render unnecessary damage. Making art can get messy. One must be emotionally available. Tensions develop. To point to an agreed-upon value that has gone missing can help identify, simplify, and resolve the problems as they come up. It also makes clear that there is an equal responsibility to own your power and take agency in the space while maintaining the contract. Know the difference between an abusive situation and the personal discomfort that this art form sometimes demands. If you strike a balance between the needs of the group and your own needs, you respect yourself and others.

As for individuals setting out to create a solo; on those days when you find yourself alone in your own head battling the demon of judgment or defeat, it's helpful and a little less lonely to pull up your values and spend some time meditating on them. The very act of doing so can remind you that perhaps you are faltering because you aren't being truthful or, on the other side of the coin, that you are judging your own ideas harshly. In which case, borrow a line of Bruce McCulloch's from the Kids In the Hall comedy troupe: "If an idea is bad, it's not your fault, it's the idea's fault." Think of it as part of the **economy** of your project because if you hammer away at yourself without remembering **generosity** as you would with others, you'll deplete your **energy** reserves and threaten your art making.

Now let's use **generosity** as a **value** and answer the earlier question asked about writing a book that gives away the lifetime's accrual of knowledge and intellectual properties that are a big part of the OYR **economy**. We prefer to view our work as an open platform where the sharing of everything we know enriches us and adds to our own knowledge base.

We feel confident that it's a combination of these tools, in our hands, within our aesthetic that have made our body of work uniquely ours. We also desire to be of service to other artists who share our passion and fascination for the theatre and to watch how they take these tools and make their own unique thing.

Since the OYR Lab began, many training labs and intensives have sprung up all around the country, a welcome change from the slim offerings of twenty years ago.

If everyone espouses the kinds of values suggested here, especially generosity, the theatre will flourish and prove a worthy devotion for generations to come.

Activity PLAY

Write down ten or more values that represent qualities you aspire to in your everyday personal life. (Blake Brooker uses ten because he says he has ten fingers to count them on and remember them by.)

Now write down the values that you would choose for a rehearsal room or in your working life. Compare the lists and see how they align or differ.

Ask a colleague or friend to do the same and spend some time in conversation to illuminate your choices.

Ask yourself how rigid or flexible your list is.

In what circumstance would you reconsider your list?

Imagine a flagrant violation of an agreed-upon value and how you might approach a resolution.

Are some values restrictive to creative freedom?

Imagine how a list of values could stomp the buzz or the fun in the room and ask yourself if that possibility is avoidable.

The exercise goes back to the question of the quality of life you wish to enjoy as an artist and a person, and might help you design a creative realm that can support that desire.

WHO DOES WHAT

Whatever the initiating idea, we have roles.

When designing the Lab all those years ago, I asked each artist to submit an application, which could be anything at all as long as it gave me a sense of who they were and how they define their art practice. I have received everything from a simple headshot, CV and cover letter to a deconstructed CD player that spit out small biographical notes, to a freshly baked cake that arrived by courier. I follow up with a phone call/interview just to insure that all of the artists have advanced study in their field.

The Lab welcomes all kinds of artists of diverse ages and practices but is not the place for beginners. Advanced study suggests a serious commitment to their chosen form, which allows for a higher level of engagement amongst the group. At this writing the oldest Labbit was a seventy-three-year-old investigative journalist with a creative writing practice, and the youngest was seventeen, from a theatre family, who had already been engaged in making theatre for ten years. We have welcomed professional musicians, architects, television actors with big careers, mid-career choreographers who tell stories, stand up comedians who dance, designers who write plays, novelists battling stage fright, graduating theatre students just setting out from post secondary life, and professors closing in on retirement.

In conducting the phone call/interview, two commonalities have been evident. The first is the number of folks who feel they need permission to begin something new, regardless of their often-impressive CVs. *(See Part One Chapter One).* The second refers to this issue of 'who does what'. It is surprisingly common to hear about creative endeavours that begin with genuine excitement and a sense of kinship only to go off the rails because of confusion over leadership and decision-making. In each instance an aesthetic attraction or idea had become split by two or more creative minds taking the ball and running with it in different directions. I have heard many stories over the years of the igniting artist's confusion and pain over giving away control of a concept precious to them, with no means of getting it back, or a director handicapped by being in the room with an artist unwilling to take direction. Let's be honest that our business involves ego and passion and is often destined for crunchy moments no matter what, so when we enter into a process with the proper discussion of roles and terms, we stand a much better chance of problem solving through those times to find the creative solution.

At OYR, our shows are initiated from a seed idea; maybe it's a motivating concept for which everyone will generate performative material, or it's an extant script, or an adaptation. It could be a song cycle in oratorio form or a full musical theatre piece. Maybe the show will explore the *ouvre* of a particular artist like Leonard Cohen, Sylvia Plath, or Anne Sexton. Whatever the initiating idea, we have roles. They do overlap and blur all the time but it is generally understood that, in our ensemble, Blake will direct, I will physically stage the work, we will engage a stage manager – and we are very lucky that as of this writing we have the very best in Johanne Deleeuw, a consummate professional who has joined the ensemble – and the actors will take full responsibility and command of their own performance within those parameters. Although each new exploration could mean a new set of guidelines and/or rotating personnel, and although we lean to an open and collaborative atmosphere, we respect these roles and terms and feel they have contributed to our longevity.

SMASH CUT FREEZE

"I'm not ready for discernment, I'm still making and…
You. Are. Judging. Me."

In 2011, I had an idea for a new show to perform with Andy Curtis and Christopher Duthie, with a score by Richard McDowell. It was a complex process. Somehow without entirely realizing it, I managed to stage the show first, then design it with the designer, Fiona Kennedy, then continue to work backwards to the writing. It was a complete reversal of the normal direction of the steps in a creating a show. Let me explain.

I had long been fascinated by the 1952 film of the Carson McCullers' stage adaptation of her novel, *The Member of the Wedding* and could never put my finger on what it was that was so unusual and captivating to me. Having watched it innumerable times since my own childhood, it wasn't until my umpteenth viewing in 2010 that I finally did some internet digging and realized I was seeing a Hollywood film starring the same cast who, when the filming began, had just finished 501 performances of the play on Broadway. On screen, the actors have the unusual quality, for film, of muscled theatricality, defying all the rules that define the difference between a stage and a film performance. Indeed these are remarkable actors who knew the difference; especially Ethel Waters sailing through her scenes like a stately ship and Julie Harris twitching and itching and wriggling her way through the tumult of adolescence. The novel and subsequent stage and film adaptations are complex, very moving, full of identity issues and the pain of exclusion and these fully realized performances were a lesson in **precision, economy, and relaxation** that only the two years of stage time had made possible.

I determined that I would honour my fascination and experiment with the film as the point of departure for a new piece, hence my choice of a title: *Smash Cut Freeze*. Purely on intuition, I assigned each actor the task of tracking, in detail, every movement of the film's three characters. Andy was to learn Ethel Waters, Christopher would follow Brandon de Wilde who played the adorably fey cousin, and I would track Julie Harris. Because I wanted to limit our work to the kitchen scenes, we had a table and three chairs, an apron, a broom, a white lace dress, and a knife as our prop, costume, and set pieces. The work was tedious — you begin to see a pattern here; commitment to possibly odious chore-like activities in the service of a bigger idea, as outlined in my Sidebar descriptions of the making of *What the Thunder Said* or *Kawasaki Exit* in chapters four and fourteen.

I hadn't imagined how tedious it would be, but as we ground our way through, a few seconds at a time, remote in hand and the film on the back wall, it became very obvious. It took a full week but finally we had a detailed sequence of everything the film actors did on screen, from the smallest gesture to the wildest outbursts. Our stage manager, Johanne Deleeuw, filmed us and OYR composer Richard McDowell stood by with what I soon noticed was not a very happy look on his face. He and I had worked and played together since our first outings as creative artists in the eighties and were very familiar and generous with one another's foibles and preferences, but I could not help but see this was something else.

Things came to a head when we ran the forty-minute sequence one afternoon and then sat to talk about what we had discovered. The actors were good-natured about the difficulty of remembering the sequence and the trickiness of keeping an eye on each other so we would stay in sync. Johanne offered her observations and finally Richard spoke up: "Denise, I don't know what you are doing but I do not like it. It's boring and totally uninteresting to me!"

I was stunned and hurt and of course felt deeply embarrassed so I asked for the room and everyone went for coffee, leaving Richard and me alone. Not really knowing where to start, I launched into a defence of my process; "This was just the first stage of my work, of course it was still nothing but a weird detailed sequence of movement, I needed to continue without feeling his ire", and finally I realized that he was kind of breaking a cardinal One Yellow Rabbit rule, so I blurted out: "I'm not ready for discernment, I'm still making and… You. Are. Judging. Me."

That **value** of not judging at the beginning is entrenched in the OYR 'mandate' for making. Richard was normally one of my closest colleagues but previous to our beginning this work, we had been through another tough workshop on a different idea, and he was also dealing with some physical pain. As he sat watching us grapple with the task at hand, his frustration and discomfort grew until it overwhelmed him and he had to say so. With my words hanging in the air between us, he thought for a moment and then a huge grin spread across his face. "You're right. I am judging you. OK. I'll stop. I won't judge you. I trust you."

There may well be times that demand a tough conversation in order to let an instigating artist know that you just don't believe in the work, or how they are going about it. Richard felt this was one of those times but my calling upon the notion of non-judgment gave him the opportunity to change his mind. He agreed to suspend his judgment of stage one of what was a complicated process and to support the ongoing work. Had we not been able to call on a value that we really believed in, his feelings would have blocked and probably derailed the project; but because we could and did, we were able to hug it out and go on. The rest of the gang came back and Richard graciously told them that he had renewed faith in my ability to see my way through the next stages of development. The team went on to analyze each physical scene for action and intention, which provided us with an entirely different storyline from the McCullers original and completed the backwards process by finally leading me to write the script itself. With everyone's ability to honour a value One Yellow Rabbit stands by, we wound up creating a successful show in a new way and continuing our collective investigation of performance theatre making. And even more importantly, Richard and I continued on as cherished colleagues working together at OYR.

Chapter Eleven

CREATING THE PERFORMANCE PLAN

Execution is the chariot of genius.
— William Blake

Concepts, Material Elements and Organizing Principles
As is by now becoming abundantly clear, One Yellow Rabbit is a Performance Theatre Ensemble and favours a structuralist approach to play-making. The arrangement of the elements in a way that encourages the viewer to compare and contrast them to derive meaning gives the play its structure. Although sometimes a narrative drive emerges, the work is almost always made this way, and plot or story is rarely the creative drive. The elements themselves are the steel and lumber that will build the architecture or the intellectual structure that the performers can enter into with the audience to explore, contemplate, and meditate on a given **theme bundle** of ideas. With that in mind, we must still start somewhere with a concept and find those **organizing principles** or elements to build with, and so must you.

Let us recap then. You have a concept that determines whether you are making a group piece or a solo. You have a clear idea of whom you want to work with and how you want to work with them. Maybe the concept is broad; say an examination of corporate and political greed, or maybe it's specific; the joy that one small event gives to one person. Perhaps you have fallen under the spell of someone else, an historical figure from some realm not your own or maybe it's a family member you have heard stories about who holds some ghostly ancestral place in your psyche.

You are so moved by this prodding psychic burr that you have determined you will gather yourself together and aim at a performance that will…that will…that will do what? Illuminate? Meditate upon? Question? Solve? Accuse? Celebrate? Warn? All of these? None of these? The questions are useful so you embrace them and find yourself in a room. You 'prepare to prepare' with your **physical practice**, you have assembled your tools and **material elements** … or have you?

Whatever it is that has brought you to this point, once you have some **materials** to work with, you are no longer reliant on pure inspiration. You can take **inventory** of all of your creative elements, place them 'side by side on your arborite table' (see chapter one sidebar) and start spinning your own gold. If your scenario concerns a specific idea, chances are that your **material resource inventory** will reveal the 'stuff" you have compiled to draw from: books, pictures, your computer Word files or your notebook chockablock with crowded notes. But let us examine the situation if you find yourself with only the intuitive emotional landscape of your own personality and no other materials to work with.

It is not unusual that an artist finds that they are haunted by some personal and intuitive longing, manifesting as a jumble of mysterious sensations and emotions. Great art has come into the world for millennia

The Lab: Caroline Sniatyski performs "All of Us."
Exploring the world of material at your fingertips, in the place where you live.

from issues of the heart, or existential longing, or suffering, but deeply personal work places you in the tricky landscape of the 'confessional'. On one hand, you may locate authentic and original aspects of yourself and your world view with intelligence, grace, and wit that will provide a thoughtful experience for an audience. On the other hand, it must be said, you run the risk of straying into sentimental or trite territory. It could be that you are struggling with those incoherent sensations because you are not yet ready to make this work!

There is only one way to find out and much like the painter needs to be in the studio to make a painting, you need to get active, find some **material elements** and put your practice and tools to work. Give yourself permission to continue the investigation, digging into your artistry, exploring inner space and asking yourself once again: Who am I now? What is it compelling me? Is this a mere study or is it worthy of an audience? Honour that intuitive drive, look around you and examine the aesthetic elements of your own life.

Mine and divine from your own shelves, closets, and cupboards and see what leaps into your hands. Scan your library, literary and musical, your images and photos, your clothing and shoes, slide open a drawer. What **pierces** you most profoundly right now? Why have you saved that broken ruler from grade one, or that robe of your great aunt's? No need yet to place a responsibility upon these elements to explain themselves or reveal how they will integrate themselves into your work, just see what speaks to you and place those objects or clothing items, that list of songs or symphonies, that poem, that novella, those **organizing principles** into some kind of container and carry it into your workroom. (See *Sign Language* sidebar, pages 143-44.)

Inventory of All Resources

As you move towards your creation period, whether you intend on devising a script from scratch or leaping off from an extant artifact, take an **inventory of all available resources**, human and non-human: the budget, the timeline, the theatre you'll be performing in, the materials, creative elements, sets and costumes necessary for rehearsal and performance, the skills and abilities of the artists involved, the ideas, and the energy.

At OYR we borrow the term '**available light**' from photography to ask ourselves what resources exist around us that we can utilize and what we will need to invent or create. Being minimalist by definition, it's a big part of our preferred aesthetic that we don't spend a great deal on sets and costumes, but if we do, they must serve the performance and the performers rather than the other way around.

Everything that will have to come into the space is noted in order to allocate time, money, and energy wisely and to keep a realistic balance between what we want and what we need. From the very beginning Blake felt strongly that the company needed its own home and The Big Secret Theatre has served as both rehearsal and performance space for almost all OYR shows, proving in many ways, an efficient model for making work. As often as possible, we layer in set and costume pieces in early days. The lights and sound are being designed and added at the same time scenes and physical vocabs are being devised, written and staged.

There is something very beautiful about rehearsing a scene and suddenly feeling the magic of the light hit you or beginning a movement section and hearing the sound design at full value for the first time. As the technical elements accrue, a heightened relationship to the text or the movement accelerates the sense of full performance values for the players and provides an advantage that traditionally happens only during tech week. We also make all of our rehearsals open, encouraging the small burst of performance energy that a guest inspires in the room and reminding ourselves that everything we are doing is eventually for an audience.

Whether you share a minimalist aesthetic or crave work that highlights a passion for design, the **inventory of all resources** is a helpful link in the chain of events that will allow you to work backwards in time from opening night. For example, what are the technical requirements? Is this a stripped back 'human being in light' piece or are there technologies that will demand a large chunk of your creative energy? Consider the impact they will have.

Devise the show you want but if your vision employs glorious technologies, make sure you factor in how much of your schedule will be gobbled up, maybe leaving other elements under rehearsed and reducing the overall effectiveness of the production on opening night. Blake uses the inventory to illuminate priorities and budgets of money, time and energy; an essential step in building a performance that will best serve the needs of the project. As William Blake reminds us, the vision of even the most brilliant artist in the world is for naught if it fails in execution.

SIGN LANGUAGE

She will do anything she feels like
She will be along. She wants to entertain.

The solo I made myself called *Sign Language* that forms the very first personal sidebar in this book started as one of those personal intuitive drives that would not leave me alone. I asked my OYR colleagues, about creating space in the calendar for me to make a solo show and they agreed. I was asked to provide a press release blurb and came up with the following statement that reveals just how vague my idea was:

Sign Language: A Physical Conversation Performed by Denise Clarke. Why do some people have to dance? What makes a choreographer? What is a dance? What the heck is Clarke trying to say? A physical conversation? What is that? Is this a dance show or a play? Will there be music? She is an actor — no? She is a dancer? Ballet? No. Modern. Not really. Exotic dancer, stripper, free-spirited nymph in chiffon? Inspired by Balanchine, Isadora, Nijinsky or Fosse? Clarke promises to dance and talk about it after. She says she will do anything she feels like. She will be alone. She wants to entertain. She wants to move people. One Yellow Rabbit says, "Why the heck not.

This was fairly glib press release nonsense that I must have hoped made my experiment sound interesting enough to attract an audience. Because experimental it was. I had one concept that I had seized upon to help me figure out what was provoking me towards a new solo creation: the piece would 'make itself' through a series of fifty repetitions. I invited one observer to each repetition, mentioning only that I was curious to see what would happen if I allowed my body rather than my intellect to make a piece of theatre. If they said they were interested, I would give them the exact time and prepare for two hours. Upon their arrival, I would lead them to a seat and explain the undertaking: an hour of improvisational movement, manipulating a series of **material elements**. I suggested it might get boring and if so they could close their eyes and nap but requested that they please stay the full hour! (I kid you not). At the end, they were welcome to ask me up to four questions or they could leave the room in silence but I wanted no opinions or general feedback. It all sounds incredibly pretentious, but I was playful and confident and somehow I had the required observer every day waiting outside the door.

However, with the rehearsal period approaching, I found I had no **material elements** to manipulate or organize my experiment around and I grew increasingly nervous. Observers were scheduled and OYR expected to present an hour of theatrical dance. Out of desperation, I paced about my house 'divining' certain objects from my closets and shelves. There was an exquisite antique silk nightgown from the 1940s that my mother had given me, a full-length gold satin skirt, a sleek little black dress, stupidly high heels, several pieces of music, a few monologues I had committed to memory, and a book of poems by Anna Swir, all of which 'put themselves' into my hands almost arbitrarily without my really understanding why or in fact caring. I packed them up and went off to begin my experiment.

During the repetitions, a certain order of events began to take place; a monologue followed by a piece of music or a poem. About ten repetitions in, I put on a never-before-played CD of Arvo Pärt's *Miserere* that I had resisted because of the massive popularity his music had enjoyed with choreographers back in the nineties. Although I too adored his music, I suppose I fancied myself using a more original or unusual choice to score my work with, but there it was in my hands, so I put it in the CD player.

Not being a Christian I didn't recognize the liturgical hymns the music is set to, but after ten days of blindly groping along a darkened hallway, I found the music moving me towards some kind of structure. At a very dramatic moment as the voices soared, a beam of sunlight shot through the high window and hit me just as I dropped to my knees. It was fantastic and funny and I found myself reacting as though a god had just made an appearance with whom I began a tentative mouthed but silent conversation that grew into a vehement argument. Although the comedy was clear, it also outlined the poignant need for some kind of spiritual conversation that both my everywoman character and me needed. The glorious music guided me towards a realization that the creative longing that had initiated the experiment was in fact an existential inquiry juxtaposed with humour, fear, and pathos. The Arvo Pärt, my mother's nightgown, the little black dress, the heels and the golden skirt, all played big into that journey and I became convinced that the arbitrary nature of my divining them as elements wasn't that arbitrary after all. *Sign Language* remains my most toured work and taught me more about myself as a person and an artist than anything else I have ever made.

Chapter Twelve

CONCEPT DEVELOPMENT

> *It's a profoundly creative act to note how the
> things in your head got there. Once you know,
> you may be able to control what else gets there.*
> — *Blake Brooker*

SITTING IN FRONT OF YOU is your concept, staring at you, waiting. Perhaps woven into and around the concept, is an **organizing principle** or two that excite or fascinate you and serve as **fetish** for the piece: a poetic strand or strands that help define the aesthetics and/or give you a way into the heart of the piece. (For example if the larger concept is the global dependence on fossil fuels, an organizing principle might be the contrasting notion of natural spring water being harvested and sold in plastic bottles made from petroleum products that are ruining the oceans of the world.) The concept has seized your curiosity but without productivity, you are standing still, completely dependent upon your imagination. **Concept development** is the act of freeing your imagination from that sole responsibility by stimulating it with information that will expand the concept beyond your own context and into universal ones.

Blake is fond of quoting the great German philosopher

Arthur Schopenhauer from *The Art of Literature*: "Reading is like thinking with someone else's head instead of one's own." He borrows this idea to research and develop a concept beyond his own context by examining it through each of four lenses: **History. Poetry. Morality. Politics.** The lenses help organize and download available knowledge surrounding your concept and lead to active specific engagement and productivity.

Lenses and Filters

Lenses are how you view the world in general. Filters are how you close in on specifics. Think about your music, your books, the podcasts you listen to, search engines you use for internet research, the radio you tune in, friends, teachers, and the list goes on. Some of these are lenses and some are filters. It could be said that the entire internet is a lens and to a lesser degree, so is your search engine of choice. As you click inward you are filtering for more and more specific information.

Pre-internet, the Library was a lens that you physically entered, and then, as you checked out the index cards or wandered into your favourite sections, you began filtering towards the information you wanted and, if you were lucky, stumbling onto unexpected gleanings. If you were most often to be found in the political science section, it was a very different gathering ground of material and ideas than if you veered straight for the poetry or fiction section. Outside of the library, if the greater lens for information about the world you lived in was strictly from reading the newspaper and watching television, you would have been gathering facts and ideas through the filters of the journalists and content providers of your papers and television channels of choice.

In 2018, it is not unusual to use social media sites as

one's main information gathering tool, which raises the question, who is the filter or source that posts what? In the creative endeavour of making something uniquely yours, you will want to think about it carefully. How did this get into my brain? Why does it matter to me?

By taking a moment to note what filters you tend towards and use on a regular basis, you understand something about yourself intellectually, poetically, morally, politically, and historically. It is easy to subscribe to a blogging platform website and browse through it daily without ever really thinking about how that filter is affecting your word view; but of course it is and may very likely be part of the aesthetic choices you make, so it makes sense to consider how and why you are absorbing your facts and fetishes!

And here again you are finding another way to determine your aesthetic preferences. If you have long admired another person, chances are you will be more inclined to take their advice for suggested reading or listening or viewing. That person functions as a filter and we can benefit from their knowledge as long as we consciously consider the context in which we are absorbing the information they lead us to.

What was your general interest in either another person or a content provider, and then what was the deeper engagement that held you? Use the 'Punctum Alert', get more specific and ask yourself what exactly you are responding to and/or accepting. What has pierced you about a song or a novel or a performance? This is gold for your own project because all great art connects to other great art. In fact it's a great idea to alert yourself to the use of whatever creative devices and aspects that affect you in any work you love and catalogue it in your **Journal of Aesthetics**.

There is a cautionary note here: as a fan of another artist you may find yourself trying to recreate what they do. If so, then Blake suggests you go all the way and undertake an in-depth study, literally copying out a novel or play that you admire, longhand, to learn how it was made. But if you intend to incorporate any of their work in your own, make sure it is acknowledged. Stay thoughtful and cognizant of how influences are affecting your work. Some artists make the actual work itself their concept. Elevator Repair Service Theatre had an interest in examining the work of F. Scott Fitzgerald's *The Great Gatsby* and wound up saying every word of it onstage in a six-hour theatrical offering. In examining and expanding your own concept, there are no rules and no limits, but think about it in its own context as well as your own. No matter how completely you are responding to something or someone else, you want to take your place as a creative artist with originality and authenticity.

Activity PLAY

1. Write down one or more intentional lenses and filters that determine how you consume content from the worlds of:

Literature and Poetry

e.g. Lens: Novels ... Filters: 19th century writers, female writers, Best Annual Book lists, Book Festivals, The New York Times Book Review, Canadian Literature, The Guardian Books, local bookstore.

Politics, *Lens: ... Filters:—*

History, *Lens: ... Filters:—*

Cinema, *Lens: ... Filters:—*

Music, *Lens: ... Filters:—*

2. Do you have any reverse or unintentional lenses or filters? e.g. I hate all Art Rock and have never therefore listened to Radiohead's music. (Too bad for you if that is the case! Full disclosure: I am a huge fan.)

3. How do your preferences influence the lenses you use and how are they useful to you or limiting to you?

Haikus and Splashing It Out

> *"When in doubt, write a haiku."*
> — *Blake Brooker*

Most folks know the basics of the Japanese poetic form: three lines, seventeen syllables most often about nature, the first line using five syllables, the second using seven, the third using five. It is a beautiful cultural form and there are specific rules if one is attempting to write a genuine haiku. But Blake borrows the form to further develop a concept.

The humble haiku can be put to work in any situation – as an observation, a thought, or an action. And like lenses, haiku reminds us of the **power of limitations**. There are a thousand directions to take when setting off on a journey of the imagination, and finding a way to begin is often overwhelming. By consciously setting limitations, like observing through one of the lenses or writing only seventeen syllables, it is easier to drive the engine of creative action.

Whether OYR is working with an extant script or 'creating from scratch', Blake uses the haiku to engage the actors in consideration of their character, to create back-story, to discover relationship to others, or to observe an aspect **historically, politically, poetically, or morally** from any point of view. These are flash studies, not an attempt to write a well-made poem but rather something to get the ball rolling and warm up the creative muscles.

In using this tool, you could labour over your seventeen syllables, deciding that they are lame or unworthy, and okay, let's just agree that they might be! The greater purpose and practice of speed writing haikus is to jolt the mind into action without judgment, introduce new ideas and angles, and make discoveries about the characters who will populate your drama.

Whether you are alone in your zone or jamming with a posse, you will be well advised to put away your 'good writer' hat and just **splash it out**, fast and dirty, saving yourself from the pain of trying to 'write well'. It is very difficult to 'write well' on command, but one can create the circumstance and atmosphere where good writing could occur and at the same time you could find yourself wandering in new territory.

The essential work here is to **develop the concept** and the **characters** and to begin the process of **material creation**. The compressed nature of the haiku forces succinct choices and distills your thoughts, providing concise bits to play with that will not hamper the work and could even enhance it – maybe even making the final cut to appear in the production. For the soloist or the group, a bank of these studies can accumulate in no time and lead to scene ideas or simply just function to inform the process beyond **curiosity** and into **productivity**.

Activity PLAY

Read ahead to the next sidebar about The Lonely Story of One Woman's Evian Bottle and then write a few haikus about your personal history with plastic water bottles. Break the rule if you want and forget about the three lines but limit yourself to the seventeen syllables. Set a time limit of fifteen minutes and challenge yourself to splash out three haikus through various lenses and from various points of view.

*The sidebar shows seventeen-syllable haikus written firstly through the **morality lens** from the point of view of a person who is conflicted about BPAs and plastics in the ocean; and secondly, a playful one, from the stance of a harsh judge.*

THE LONELY STORY OF ONE WOMAN'S EVIAN BOTTLE

"Let's examine this plastic bottle through the history lens first."

During the Lab in a discussion about concepts and developing them, a Labbit once asked Blake to demonstrate the use of the Lenses and Filters. He looked at the plastic Evian water bottle in her hand and began; "Okay, let's say we are going to devise a piece of performance theatre about this water bottle."

Everyone stared at him, their faces drawing a blank on what could possibly be of theatrical interest in a crappy plastic water bottle. He went on, "Let's examine this plastic bottle through the **history** lens first." What at first seemed like a banal suggestion suddenly leapt to life and the group immediately began firing information and questions back and forth. How long have humans carried water about? Prehistoric peoples carried water in bladders and horns but what were the first manufactured water containers? What was the history of plastic? In minutes, the concept of the plastic water bottle was exciting interest and energized discussion.

Blake continued, inviting the group to write haikus from the first person point of view about their own history with these bottles. The compressed seventeen-syllable stories bloomed with potential: homemade bongs, personal disasters, picnics, the desperate rationing of just such a bottle found in the woods on a camping trip gone wrong.

Someone finished reading his back to the gang with a witty but macabre lazzi (comedic routine) of breaking his own neck accompanied by the sound of the bottle being crushed. The Labbit whose bottle it was, admitted to her moral shame for even having it in her hands. The concept had become loaded, made quickly evident when viewed through the lenses of **history, poetics, morality, and politics** and everyone agreed; one plastic water bottle had enormous energy and fascinating and provocative potential for theatrical exploration about the environment and the oil and gas industry, with side stories of personal charm and humour.

The example of how to activate your concept was clear and by the end of the session, the gang were loathe to let go the show concept which they called, amusingly: The Lonely Story of One Woman's Evian Bottle.

Evian bottle haiku written firstly through the morality lens from the point of view of a person who is conflicted about both BPAs and plastics in the ocean, and so is refilling a plastic bottle to drink from, hoping to reduce, recyle and reuse:

> To offset my shame,
> I will risk rotting my brain
> and reuse this thing.

Here's one from the moral stance of a harsh judge who feels there should have been no purchase of water in a bottle in the first place.

> Go ahead loser
> Fill the oceans with plastic
> Who cares? You're thirsty.

Chapter Thirteen

HARNESSING THE POWER OF LIMITATIONS

WHETHER YOU FAVOUR WESTERN dramaturgical play-making techniques and set about writing exposition, conflict, rising action, climax, falling action and resolution, or prefer to mine from **personal aesthetic** for a more structuralist performance creation, specific studies can serve to flesh out characters, motivate plot and story points, or build innovative springboards into scenes as you build your manuscript.

Probably because he has written many plays and has experienced the writer's block that can bring all activity to a demoralizing halt, Blake Brooker has many other strategies for devising text by harnessing the powers of limitations, either sitting alone in the playwright's chair or directing a group process.

As previously stated, when the muse is guiding your hand in full creative flight, you can get your thoughts down and all is well, but when inspiration is nowhere to be found and you're stuck staring at that enemy – the blank page – you need the big secret power tool of forward momentum. And so, in no particular order, here are Blake's big secret power tools of forward momentum.

Questions and the Poetics of Action

> *Ask your character questions and*
> *watch them grow like crystals.*
> — Blake Brooker

You have waded into the development of the *Dramatis Personae* or the persons of the drama. As you begin to place them in your story or your narrative, linear or fractured, you want to find out who they are, what they do, and why. Many novelists talk about their delight while writing their story, of allowing the characters to go in their own direction, throwing the notion of the careful outline out the window. If you ask a character **questions**, demanding active answers, they might surprise you and once again liberate your imagination from the sole responsibility of charting all the paths.

In everyday life when someone asks you a question, you will respond in a few ways. A pleasant, "Hi, how are you?" is easily answered with a two-word reply; "Fine thanks." But when someone goes beyond that with a thoughtful question that makes them seem genuinely interested, you may find yourself opening up and telling them something you wouldn't have without their prompting. Conversely, what about the times when you are not interested in sharing with another individual and their questions seem to intrude into your privacy? You find yourself evading the question or outright lying in response.

Both are rich and fertile grounds to seed your character's personality traits, likes and dislikes, secrets and passions. Once you have even a vague idea of how they live in your story, place a character in time/space and put them to work answering a list of five to ten questions. They might just 'answer their way' into a more fleshed-out character

HARNESSING POWER   159

*The Lab: Alexandria Inkster performs "Mama Lives in the Sun Now."
Bringing characters into unexpected scenarios and possibilities.*

with specificities and quirks that bring them uniquely to life and introduce unexpected scenarios and possibilities; even more so if there is a team of creators in the room divvying up the roles of interrogator and interrogated. After all, the only thing better than one excited creative mind is several of them, all contributing to the '**Hive Mind**' of the project at hand.

The Rival and Actions

A character is beginning to take shape, perhaps with some descriptive and observational haikus through the four lenses. They exist in relationship to what: the world, their family, a situation? You have questioned them and received their answers in a flash survey that has provided you with some information about their existence. Is it smooth sailing or do they have tensions stretching them into a conflict, always of interest to the outside viewer.

It's one of those deeply human things that we find ourselves fascinated by the quandaries and problems of others. If you want to create a little something for your characters to bump up against, nothing spices things up better than a rival to energize and add dimensional conflict to the story. The rival has attributes that are problematic; they have acted in some way that has offended, whether they know it or not.

It could be that just by living in the same world they have wounded your character, or more nefariously, they have set out to do mischief with the intent to harm. Once you have that rival in mind; run them through the same cycle of descriptive haikus and questions and answers or use one more spoke in the wheel of material creation and splash out a **list of actions**. For example here are five actions from an imaginary workplace rival:

> I compare myself to her and I am jealous. I steal her phone. I text flirtatious messages to our boss. I place her phone back on her desk when no one is watching. I go to the men's room, wash my hands and smile at myself in the mirror.

This bold tack of finding **rivals** and **actions** for any character can deliver you right into the heart of a conflict, and the rival and their actions needn't just be in the realm of the human being. It's your call on how outrageous or subtle the actions are. There is some actual historical precedence for inanimate objects being prosecuted for doing a human harm, one of the earliest being an ancient Greek statue referred to in Plato's *The Laws*. Theagenes the Boxer was rumoured to be the son of Hercules and celebrated

*The Lab: Pamela Tzeng performs "Meditation on the End"
Stumbling onto a fascinating character not even necessarily human.*

for his many victories as an Olympian, but he had some disgruntled rivals, one of whom was not content to let even Theagene's death be the end of it. When a statue was erected in the famous boxer's memory, every night his rival visited to exact his revenge by whipping its bronze back, until one night the statue toppled over and killed him. Bizarrely, his sons prosecuted the statue for their father's murder, and more weirdly, they won their case and the statue was thrown into the sea!

Imagine the **actions** the statue of Theagenes might list:

> I look down at the pathetic man whipping me. I remember the shape of his wife's hips. I remember breaking his nose in a match when we boxed. I laugh at his effort to take revenge on my bronze back. I ask the gods to inch me slowly off my pedestal.

Any one of these **actions** arrived at quickly can open a door. The story and the plot bloom, the characters grow, our curiosity and our creativity become productive and if we're lucky, we stumble onto a fascinating character not even necessarily human.

Photographs

> *Transport yourself to the bedroom of someone in your story. Beside their bed is a nightstand and it has a drawer. At the very back you find a special secret stash of photographs…*
> — Blake Brooker

Describing photographs is another highly specific exercise with a limitation that Blake often challenges the ensemble to undertake. To introduce the concept and give an example of how quickly one can enter into the world of the character through an imagined snapshot of their life, let's take a shortcut and look at some imagined photos.

The first is a Polaroid photo, a close up of a small boy looking unhappily into the camera's eye. Just over his shoulder is an adult feminine hand reaching into the frame and holding a bottle of Orange Crush pop. The hand has rings on every finger and a gold watch on the wrist. The child has black curls and big brown eyes, brimming with tears. His bottom lip is pushed out and it seems he is about to burst into tears. His Metallica tee-shirt is much too big and he pulls at the neck of it.

The second photograph is what appears to be a family portrait cut from a contact sheet with the word 'Sears' and the date 1971 stamped on the back. There is a mother, father, two girls, and a pubescent male who seems to be the same boy from the first photo. He stands sullenly in the

*The Lab: Russell Wustenberg performs "The Moons of Saturn."
Transported by a photograph.*

middle between the father and the mother whose hands reveal that she is the owner of the gold watch and the many rings. She is painfully thin and does not look well, but is smiling broadly. The father is very tall and handsome, but his smile is unconvincing. They are a bi-racial family and the two daughters in the shot are blonde and blue-eyed identical twins who look as though they are in their early teens. The mother and daughters are carefully made up and all wear the same shiny pale pink lip-gloss. Everyone is dressed and coiffed immaculately but the photo has a sense of tragedy to it.

A third photo is a shot of our same sullen youth now all grown up and looking to be in his late thirties, slouched in a chair, legs crossed, playing a guitar. His hair is a beautifully styled pompadour with a long black curl drooping over his forehead and he is wearing a red leather jacket. A little girl wearing a white communion dress and veil stands beside him, beaming and holding a piece of cake with a lit candle. On the back it says in blue ink, "Papa's 40th! 1997." Written in pencil in brackets underneath is written "and my communion!!!"

The photographs begin to form a narrative on their own. They are engrossing to write and provide just enough tantalizing detail that you can telescope in or out of them to expand that narrative. To hear them read aloud also allows the listener to imagine beyond just the image. Blake uses the photographs in a few different ways.

If the ensemble is staging an extant script, he asks each actor to absorb what they can from a few readings and explore backstory possibilities by writing their own series of photographs from the bedside drawer of the character they will play. If the ensemble is devising a project, the photos are written to invent or develop character and story and will go into the performative material pool, possibly to be used to create monologues or scenes. The photographs are often compelling and mysterious. Reading them aloud to each other creates an unfolding universe that can be surprising or whimsical and takes full advantage of the hive mind.

It is just as marvelously useful for the solo creator to open that imaginary nightstand drawer and envision a handful of photographs. It doesn't matter if your story is a true tale, a personal story featuring people in your life, a wild invention from your deepest intuitive fancy or a well-made play based on historical fact. Describing a snapshot is an excellent way to energize and entertain yourself and might also lead to a goldmine you hadn't yet discovered.

Letters

Letters are another rich vein to tap. Writing a letter to someone else in your narrative or even to an unseen person in the story might also lead to fresh details. Got a cruel offstage father? A generous lover left forever behind? An over-protective mom? Write them a letter to find out if there are any unconscious stones to roll off and reveal new information.

It is a fantastic discovery as a writer or an actor to find oneself stumbling onto completely playable emotions and situations by writing a letter to someone either merely mentioned in the script or to another character with whom you haven't yet connected. Like the **haikus**, the **questions**, the **actions**, and the **photographs**, there is much to mine from imagined correspondences between real or made up acquaintances.

Monologues, Dialogues, and Other Scene Ideas

With the pool of material growing and the story, plot, and characters taking shape, make sure you **name each study**, write it down on a Post-it note and stick it on the wall. At OYR, just as in countless other writing rooms, coloured Post-its, written on with thick sharpies, cover our wall and give us something to gaze upon when we reconvene at the central table to share stuff and continue discussions. (You may prefer to just write things down on the whiteboard or spread your scenes and ideas on a floor or table but for our purposes here, we'll use the good old Post-it as our stand in for a device that allows us to name and see what we have.)

The Post-its serve the same purpose that the crime wall does in the criminal procedural television shows and films you might be familiar with; a visual journal of discoveries made as the investigation continues. Each day a few more go up, some come down, some move over to the 'maybe file' and as more information comes to light, the individual or the group can see the progress and move closer to solving the mystery, in our case, "What happens in this piece of theatre?"

One is wise to use the computer to keep organized files

of all written material, but nothing takes the place of being able to sit together and look at all the ideas and material in one spot, keeping track of where you're at while stoking the forward momentum.

As the stuff gets shared, scene ideas will occur and the head writer, director, or you as the sole creator, can assign monologues, dialogues, trialogues, and so on. Blake often gets the beehive busy by dividing the group into twos and threes to write together. Sometimes a player will feel an affinity for something and write a scene to offer the group on their own volition.

All these tools are equally applicable to the sole writer or the posse. And not to forget that should you care to, you can be still be creating **physical vocabs** and **musical files** or songs, also named on their own colour-coded Post-it and stuck up on the wall. Eventually your schedule will demand you cease the material creation phase, which has provided you with a rich pool of performative stuff to discern from, and the project moves into the next phases of **selection** and **arrangement**.

Activity PLAY

1. Think about someone imaginary or real. Open that nightstand drawer beside their bed. Reach in and pull out a small stack of six photographs. Describe them.

2. Now read what you've written and choose a person or object mentioned in the photos. Write three observational haikus about them or it using first, second, or third person point of view (POV).

3. Ask them five questions.

4. Write their answers.

5. Ask them five more questions.

6. Write their evasions to these five questions.

7. Invent a rival for this person you've plucked from your photos. Write four haikus describing the rival. One about their history. One about their politics. One about their creative or poetic nature. One about their morality. Use any POV you choose.

8. Write a list of actions of the rival. Write a list of actions of the original person.

9. Have the original person write a letter to the rival.

This may take you a few hours to complete but will introduce you to how deliciously effective it is to 'trick yourself' into creating a lot of material and learning a great deal about both yourself and the subjects you are inventing.

*Expand or contract the Activity, change the rules, shift the point of view but remember the power of limitations and stay playful. These studies may only be a warm up or they may lead to other scene ideas. Craft them to find out everything you can **historically, morally, politically, and poetically** and to establish context, conflicts, relationships and specific character traits and details all of which will bring depth, richness, and originality to your scripted scenes.*

With Andy Curtis, Onalea Gilbertson, and Michael Green.

SYLVIA PLATH MUST NOT DIE

The OYR Ensemble has a passion for building shows that highlight the poetry of poets we love. Making *Sylvia Plath Must Not Die* in 2008, was the illumination of the two so called 'suicide poets' Sylvia Plath and Anne Sexton, confessional innovators who helped change 20th century poetry after meeting in their mentor Robert Lowell's class. Onalea Gilbertson played Plath, with Michael Green as her equally famous poet husband, Ted Hughes. I played Sexton with Andy Curtis as my husband Kayo and Blake directed.

Anne Sexton's work came up one day when we were working on a wildly different project with the Canadian rock band, The Rheostatics. Dave Bidini, the rocker writer of the book, *Five Hole, Tales of Hockey Erotica* invited us to stage and perform it with himself and his band mates. Who could say no to a show about sex, rock and roll, and hockey, and to playing beside one of Canada's finest and most original rock bands? Certainly not us, so we jumped aboard and got to work. On the first day, we cracked open Dave's book to find a quote from Anne Sexton. I was very familiar with her work and mentioned her affinity and suicidal connection to Plath, adding that I preferred her poems to Plath's. Onalea leapt to Plath's defence stating that she most definitely was a fan of the latter. It led to a little sidebar activity with Blake's asking us each to find a few poems of both poets to read for a 'poet-off' mini contest the next day, which we were tickled to do and eventually resulted in the concept of doing a show about them the following year.

When that process began, Blake picked up where we left off and it was decided that Onalea and I would curate and read several poems from each poet's *oeuvre* and Michael would read a few of Ted Hughes' poems to contextualize his relationship with Plath.

The 'readings' were exciting but it was soon obvious that the project presented a big challenge in how to approach their friendship and the macabre death wish they shared without falling into tricky territory. We were searching for a suitable way to theatricalize these dense and charged poems, especially Plath's, which are famously impenetrable at times and loaded with difficult imagery. How to 'give' them without exhausting the audience and overtaxing their ability to absorb the power of the writing? More than anything, our show had to bring these women and their husbands to life with grace and humour in a way that opened sympathetic ears to what might be construed as too painful, strange, or clichéd for the listener. The confessional movement in 20th century poetry had opened the doors to much overwrought writing which had almost become a cliché, and although we Rabbits were hyper-conscious of that territory, we had tremendous passion for these two original poets and wished to effectively

Photos: Trudie Lee

bring their brilliant work to our audience. We had their poems and the connections between them to draw on, but little else.

The methods described in chapters twelve and thirteen were almost immediately implemented. Blake charged us to look through our lenses at their moral, political, and poetic histories: the state of women's rights and mental healthcare, and of poetry itself in the era in which they lived and wrote, the trickiness of their married lives, and the sorrowful way they chose to die. We combed their biographies and journals. Confessional poetry was a radical new movement in the late 1950s, which emphasized the first person narrative. Plath and Sexton drew on the details of early family life, love and marriage, motherhood, mental illness, institutionalization, and suicide to write in what were, for the times, brand new ways. Our organizing principle was to curate the poems in those biographical categories.

We wrote haikus as, about, and to our characters, exploring our own relationships to them, and theirs to each other. Physical studies allowed us to play into the sensual worlds the two women shared with their husbands and we constructed a sequence of the couples dancing together to jazz music of the era that became our opening. But finally we felt that less movement and more photographic-like tableaux were necessary to relax them all *in situ* for imagined conversations that would set up the poems. Blake had two old Adirondack chairs prepared as the only set pieces. Onalea and I wrote letters that led to dialogues with one another as Sexton and Plath, comparing notes on McLean Hospital where both poets had been confined. We lounged in our chairs smoking and amusing/horrifying each other as we traded our poems about the experience. We all invented photographs inspired by images and lines of the poems. For example, Ted Hughes has many beautiful poems about the natural world so Blake wrote a photograph that inspired a scene of a fictionalized fishing trip during which the two men talked about the complications of loving and being married to brilliant but mentally unstable women.

Sexton won the Pulitzer and although she had plenty of detractors, was literally a rock star of her era, giving wild readings for huge audiences, often backed by her band, *Her Kind*. Sadly, Plath became hugely read only after her death. Both women were important female voices in the mid-20th century, often startling the status quo with their uncompromised intelligence, sexuality, humour, and unmasked rage. Our conjured exchanges between all four characters helped set up the context in which the audience could hear the poems in a respectful, occasionally funny and alluring theatrical setting that examined their tragic deaths, yet honoured the courage and fierce life force that drove Plath and Sexton and yielded such genre-defining poetry.

Chapter Fourteen

MATERIAL SURVEY AND ARRANGEMENT

First Draft of the Performance Plan
A note here about the terms **performance plan** and **script**. Quite simply, as a confirmed structuralist, Blake Brooker prefers the term **performance plan**. It serves the same purpose that a **script** does but better describes all the mediums at work as the performance artifact comes together, and it reflects his definition of performance theatre that places the players and the playing first in his aesthetic determinations.

Understanding the allocation of resources, as covered in chapter five, determines the length of time you need to make a new work. The more resources, the longer the creation period, but once you are no longer afforded the luxury of time for **concept development** and **material creation**, you must respectfully put aside Rainer Maria Rilke's beautiful lines of advice to the young poet to 'embrace the questions' (see chapter one), for now the process of **discernment** and finding dramatic solutions begins.

With opening night soon to occur you will be delivered of the whole point of your endeavor: presentation of your creative identity, which will answer the question "Who are you now?" with the answer "This is who I am." The time has finally come to 'judge' the material and to connect things. As a formal exercise, this goes beyond a simple 'thumbs up or down', although of course you may occasionally just decide to cut something purely according to your aesthetic preferences. The job now is to bring it all together in a coherent first draft **performance plan** or **script**.

The seasoned playwright has their own methods and often works to an outline that might render this conversation moot; there are as many schools of play writing as there are playwrights, all to be honoured and learned from. But if you have been following along with the methods and methodologies put forward here, then you may be staring at a whiteboard filled with Post-its that represent your constructed content. For the most part, the scenes that needed writing have been written and you may well have an idea how it all goes together, but just as likely you may be grappling with that very thing and facing another whole set of creative decisions.

A lot of blood, sweat, and tears have gotten you this far and so it's not a bad idea to once more remind yourself of the big picture. What is the purpose of this work? To soothe, alarm, amuse, entertain, move, provoke, seduce, warn, convince, elegize, or illuminate? All of these? Some of these? None of these? Using the accepted definitions of the terms, what is the overall style of your presentation? Absurd? Classical? Are you jumping between postmodernism and naturalism? Is that a conscious decision or do you even care?

Blake suggests refreshing yourself with everything compiled thus far, by conducting a **material survey**. Be on the alert for **punctums**. What stands out for you and why? Think about your **organizing principles** and let them help you arrange the order of those Post-its on your wall in a timeline of sorts: a beginning, middle, and end. A great tool for activating this part of your brain are two more questions: **What happens first? What happens next?**

Whether you are clear on the events of your story and you are making a well-made play, or you intend your work to be an imagist abstraction with a fractured narrative deconstructed and reconstructed to your liking; onstage one 'thing' will happen after another and there may be a more or less successful arrangement of those 'things'. As you are the maestro of this performance creation, it falls to you to arrange the sequence of all your elements and events so that they best serve both your concept/piece/play and your audience.

Your intuitive intelligence, instincts, and aesthetics now guide your hand in determining how you wish the information to unfold and land in the viewers' field of perception and what tempo/dynamics are at play to keep them engaged. If while conducting your survey you find yourself leaning away from an element, just move it out of your field of vision but keep it in the 'maybe' file.

Stranger things have happened than the late rediscovery of a discarded bit of text, music, or movement that works perfectly to fill a void. Name any element obviously missing with a place holder Post-it and put it in sequence. Be conscious that much of your work now will involve **transitions.** At OYR we consider the transition to be a golden opportunity for performance, so much so that we also use it as a verb, 'to transish' but more about that in the next chapter.

You would get no argument here about the inclusion of choreographic motifs in the **performance plan** but it may be valuable to ask oneself how the movement serves the overall piece. Does it counter or illuminate what is being said? Does it exist to compel the narrative non-verbally or have you designed it as a *divertissement*? The classical ballet term 'divertissement' refers to an entertaining diversion of incidental dances, outside of the story line, that highlight the talent of the dancers. The ballet is an obvious arena for viewing virtuosity, because, after all, the technical expertise of the dancers is an enormous part of the experience.

In the performance creation you are making, a virtuosic turn is never a bad thing unless it begins to feels like an interruption in the overall flow of the ideas and meaning, so take care to place it with a beautiful set up. Startling your viewers with a moment of virtuosic delight that keeps them guessing can be tremendously effective, so long as you think about it in the context of the other objectives and intentions you are striving to deliver, and you feel confident that there is a payoff.

A payoff? It is a subjective term but let's agree that it can be irritating as a viewer to invest in a performance only to be left scratching your head trying to interpret elements left dangling. Delight, surprise, challenge, and 'play up' to your audience always, but confuse or bore them at your peril.

What about the use of repetition? Repetition can provide the viewer with the pleasure of seeing something that having been introduced, reappears in another context like a **cadeau** thanking them for their attention. They can compare and contrast what they are seeing repeated and derive further meaning. But taken too far, repetition can feel like a starkly aggressive act on the part of the performer that traps the viewer. The postmodern performance artists of the 1980s often relied on this kind of device to drive home their intent with bludgeoning overstatement. There is a balance somewhere between the two and you might wisely frame it by asking yourself how much you care about the audience? Maybe you are a passionate postmodernist and you are willing to risk alienating your audience at times in order to stay true to your own voice and aesthetics. This is a chance you must be willing to take if aesthetic values and preferences have driven your work, or if you are determined to make something radically new that eschews catering in any way to expectations. But you don't have to sacrifice all your preferences if you balance them with dynamic considerations and the offer of an occasional *cadeau* that rewards and welcomes the audience back in.

Then again, art history is loaded with extreme aesthetic choices that initially rattled the viewers and inspired fear and loathing but with time went on to be acknowledged masterpieces. Vaslav Nijinsky and Igor Stravinsky's ballet, *The Rite of Spring* caused a near riot when it premiered at the Paris Opera in 1913. It was a coin-toss which element the audience hated more, the choreography or the music – both striking examples of the modernism then sweeping the Parisienne art world. It's a fantastic tale of passionate response that initially left the creators, Nijinsky and Stravinsky, sneered at and ridiculed. Nijinsky slowly went mad until he became institutionalized, but Stravinsky went on to become the foremost contemporary composer of his day. *The Rite of Spring* is still regularly performed by orchestras and often reinterpreted by choreographers. One rejoices in imagining the two artists overcoming all odds and seeing their stunning work through to completion, outlasting their critics and creating a 20th century masterpiece.

Dynamic Intensity

But, back to success in the 21st century. Ever been to a show where everyone is shouting and bombastic the whole time? Or the tempo of the performance is relentlessly slow and pedantic? Fill in the blank with your own critical take on why something was boring, tedious, predictable, or unpleasantly exhausting. Chances are very good that the creator did not intend on that result but just somehow missed it either in the construction or the execution. The **dynamic intensity** of each element is important to consider. Imagine a graph with the minutes of your show charted along the horizontal line at the bottom and the dynamic intensity running up the vertical line. Greater dynamic intensity referring to more volume, faster tempos, passion, rising action, climax and lesser dynamic intensity to exposition, quiet contemplative scenes, slow tempos, stillness.

It's a rough and general visualization that will alert you to the overall rhythm of your show. Check for too many dynamically similar scenes following one another, or high-intensity scenes followed by low so that your graph marches up and down between markers in a regular pattern. Both of these examples are a danger if you hope to surprise your audience. Predictability is deadly in the theatre and this rather blunt exercise might come in handy to help you avoid it and keep things dynamically interesting, surprising, and engaging.

Narrowing in on Discernment and Decisions

As you finesse an arrangement and order of things, you may become overwhelmed, but take heart in the intuitive instinct and make bold choices. When John Murrell, taught at the OYR Lab, he was asked one day by one of the participants how he knew whether or not he was making the right choice when it came to this task of finding an order and putting together all the disparate elements that make up a script. He answered with a discussion of the voice inside which he calls, 'the gadget'. He mimed a small dial in the centre of his chest and turned it as one would a combination lock. "You feel it click into place and you go with it." It was a charming bit of wisdom that meant there is no way to know for certain if you are making the right decision or choice about something other than to honour your intuitive impulses. It might also be the defining mark of the artist; someone who has an instinct for creation, listens to intuition, and follows it through with actions until they feel they have completed the task. Decisions simply have to be made or one is paralyzed and standing still.

My own father handed down a very valuable tool to me when I was sixteen years old and quite certain that I would become a working artist and a responsible member of society without any further formal education. He asked how I proposed to go about that. "I don't know," I admitted, "there's so many things to decide, I don't know where to start." My dad looked at me over his cup of coffee and said: "Don't be afraid to make a decision. Try your best for as long as you can. If it doesn't work out, you can always change your mind and make another one." It kicked open the door to my creative life because it suggested a strategy for action. It had oxygen, possibility, and energy. I could proceed, I could investigate my intuitions, my instincts, I could take aesthetic risks and maybe I would succeed, maybe I'd fail. Implicitly the onus was on me to try for success: I needed to figure out who I was, what I wanted, why I wanted it and decide how to get it, *but* if the decision became a monkey on my back, if it painted me into some permanent bad corner, if I failed, I could then change my mind? That was it. Freedom! No more paralysis!

Final Draft

The dramaturgical path to the **final draft** is very difficult to undertake in a group and is best left to a final arbiter and their dramaturge of choice, as was suggested in chapter ten. If you have instigated this project with the intention of being responsible for that draft, be mindful that if you ask for too many opinions, you will get them.

Unless you are utterly committed to the collective creation process and have set it up from the beginning, it is challenging to absorb and execute disparate notes from too many sources. Many a writer has suffered through a workshop of their play, seeing it dismantled and put back together by a dramaturge, a director, and a table of actors. In such cases the playwright is expected to listen and implement notes with an open mind and heart but it is rarely easy to allow others to decide on how your play should read.

The result might be worth the pain if you are invested in that style and scale of theatre-making and are assured of a production. If you are on that path, hopefully you will find yourself working with an excellent and sensitive dramaturge, which can be tremendously rewarding, so hats off and good luck! Many of these techniques will apply all the way towards that workshop. But no matter if you are aiming for Broadway or your own boutique theatre, it remains the case that you must follow your own instincts and fearlessly ply your own aesthetics to make choices or you run the risk of making art by committee.

Consider this. It could be that you are a brilliant creator and that you have something very original and unique to contribute to the culture at large. You will only know if that is true if you step into the arena, put yourself on the line and do your best work in which case, even if you fail, there is no shame. The shame would be in never having tried, so take a chance on yourself. You will find your posse of truth speakers who you genuinely trust to help you understand how successful or undeniable your efforts have been, but in the big picture you must be the artist you are if you want to make an honest and meaningful body of work worthy of the effort.

Activity PLAY

The Night Table Drawer Performance Plan

Study for a short Imagist piece

1. If you completed the writing activity suggested at the end of chapter twelve, then you will have haikus, photographs, questions, answers and observations available to you. Name each one on a colour-coded Post-it. Write down a few musical ideas on another colour of Post-it. If you like, imagine a movement phrase or two and do the same. Put them all up on a wall in their colour categories. You may prefer to lay out your materials in another manner, but do take a material survey of everything you wrote.

2. Ask yourself: **What happens first?** Choose a Post-it that answers the question and place it on an adjoining wall to begin this draft of your performance plan.

3. Ask yourself: **What happens next?** Continue creating an order of things, each time repeating the question, curating your arrangement according to your intuitive impulse.

4. Look for additional scene ideas and/or transitions that would flesh out this draft, name them, and insert them in sequence.

5. Cut and paste and add stage directions until you have a readable draft of this short Imagist experiment. Read it out loud. Do a dynamic test graph either for real or in your mind to examine rhythm.

6. **Play** with it. Re-arrange it. Edit it. Assess the potential application of this straight-forward method for taking your developed concept into a draft.

Photo: Trudie Lee

KAWASAKI EXIT

The OYR body of work represents a huge cross section of styles being guided by the creative desires of the ensemble. From surrealistic comedies, dance dramas, extant plays, oratorios, musicals and cabaret, to illuminations of poets and poetry, adaptations and investigative salons, the work is always diverse but for the repeated emphasis on performance and performers. Driven by a minimalist preference, the limited resources available to the company at its inception, the punk rock ethos of the early eighties and the desire to see empowered players onstage in **undeniable** presentations (see Chapter 5 Precision, Economy and Relaxation) we set ourselves **NO RULES, NO LIMITS** on what it was we might choose as an instigating concept. In 2011 Blake constructed a truly remarkable and unique piece for the ensemble called *Kawasaki Exit*. The story of how the show happened provides a fascinating look at an engaged artist in the full flush of his creative power who opened a door for himself that took the company into a whole new world.

When OYR was making *Sylvia Plath Must Not Die,* Blake invented an exercise for us that in the end he would not use but which stayed with him. He had read a *Harpers* magazine article about the Japanese cultural phenomenon of 'suicide clubs', whose members found one or two others online and got together to take their own lives. Bizarrely, a common method included driving to a remote spot, lighting a small hibachi barbeque in a car, drinking vodka and swallowing pills to do the tragic deed. Blake had imagined a sensory exercise of playacting just such a ritual to help the ensemble imagine the suicides of the poets Plath and Anne Sexton, but ultimately, their circumstances were so different that he changed his mind and never even told us about it until two years later.

Not long later after finishing a tour of the Plath show in Toronto, Michael Green, Blake and I were sitting in the airport bar awaiting our flight, chatting about all manner of things including death by suicide, when Blake casually mentioned the unused exercise. He described the *Harpers* article and how it had bloomed in his mind as a full piece of theatre about a terminally ill man living in Kawasaki who wanted to end his life but was faced with the unwanted dilemma of a wife determined to join him. Fascinated, Michael and I listened as he told us his play, which was woven around the suicide clubs he had read about and concerned this dying man's poignant solution for keeping his beloved wife alive. The play would take place in real time, in a car, half in phonetic Japanese then the story would reverse in English. There would be a third person in the car who would turn out to be an actor hired by the husband to insure his wife did not die. It would be funny and sad and mysterious.

He had found, as he always does, some **organizing principles**, talismanic **fetishes** that inspire the structure and the poetics to build around. For *Kawasaki Exit*, he remembered a Japanese vodka he drank as a young man, called Come Back Salmon. He loved the symmetry of salmon swimming out to sea to live and back to spawn and die. He also thought about the symmetry of a small square of origami paper folded in on itself to make a bird, another creature that just flies away. His third fetish was a Japanese puzzle box, a beautiful object seemingly impossible to get into which, if solved, opens in thrilling ways to reveal a treasure. Michael and I loved and feared the whole thing immediately. Learn and speak phonetic Japanese while bringing full emotional verity to a 'dramedy' about suicide and love? Okay. Let's go.

Blake did go on to write the play like a puzzle box in epigrammatic sentences that revealed the couples' bantering affection as they drove through the suburbs of Kawasaki to pick up the third person, but kept the audience guessing about what was going on right up to the climactic act. Our challenge was to speak the text naturalistically, in Japanese, with enough space for the subtitles to be read and the laughs to land while playing the subtext in a buoyant and enigmatic way. Once the audience unlocked the puzzle at the end of the first act, we reversed every pedestrian action they had observed us use, in a precise physical rewind of the story, movement and text, only in English!

Blake's structuralist aesthetic inspired the symmetrical nature of the work and resulted in strangely funny yet beautiful language that plumbed complex emotions with subtlety and verity. Andy Curtis, Patrick MacEachern, and I worked our way through the painful and slow process of learning the Japanese, wonderfully translated by Manami Hara, and were rewarded with an amazing experience as players. Blake went on to write another non-English comedy, *Munich* Now, in German, calling the project his Tangled Tongue series. He has often humbled the ensemble by stating his belief that we were among the finest performing theatre ensembles in the English-speaking world, and always challenged himself and us with the example of the Cleveland Symphony's aspiration to play the world's most difficult repertoire. *Kawasaki Exit* put all that to the test in every way.

Chapter Fifteen

FINAL PRESENTATION

The Water Column

In his compositions for the stage, Blake draws inspiration from a tool often used in aquatic environmental studies: a conceptual column of water in a lake, stream or ocean examining the stratification from surface to sediment, called a water column. Everything is important and watchable for scientists in the water column. All activity and all elements within that very specific visual field are taken into account and analyzed. Blake analyzes the 'ecology' of the stage as the scientist does a water column, and he finds in this organic model a metaphor for how he determines that everything onstage is watchable. From the grid to the deck, he floods the space with light and shadow, arranging set elements so that the actors can flow in and around them, while making sure that as the timeline of the piece of theatre elapses, the dramatic highs and lows, the movement and stillness, the volumes and tempos are all balanced in an engaging rhythm.

Entrances and exits are an enormous part of the rhythm of a show. OYR original creations tend to limit them, showing a decided preference for leaving the players onstage and visible for much of the action unless it is dramatically necessary to have them gone. As is by now very clear, a strong choreographic element is also at play and scenes are arranged so they are kinesthetically interesting and connected in a coherent way using the all-important **transition**, referred to in the last chapter. To pay equal attention to how the players 'transish', styling them with **precision** and **economy** from one place to another, adds to the overall aesthetic realization. **Everything is watchable!** The players take command of the stage and control the emotional intention and flow of the information so that the production has an authoritative and at the same time **relaxed** presentation. By **relaxed**, there is not a suggestion that the performance be given casually, but rather that even in the most physically or emotionally difficult scenes the actors appear effortless, which OYR believes invites the audience in and holds them.

For a deeper understanding of **relaxation** both in process and onstage, refer to chapter two.

(A further note here on the word '**relaxed**'. In the parlance of the developing theatrical lexicon we use in 2018, the notion of the 'Relaxed Performance' has come to mean a show that has been scheduled to welcome individuals living with Autism Spectrum Disorder, Dementia, Sensory Disorders, those who have small children or any other condition that might normally inhibit their inclusion in the audience. The house lights are left on a low level and startling technical cues are tempered to be less shocking. Everyone shifts their normal expectation of silence in the audience, and/or comings and goings in the house, along with other considerations so that the theatre can accommodate any and all needs. A fantastic idea whose time has come!)

The lighting design also plays a big part of the transitions, signalling shifts in mood and thought and creating

The Lab: Alexandra Dawkins performs "DaVinci."
Exploring a full dynamic range of emotion.

lighting states from the most nuanced breakup to the boldest outline of boxed white light, to no light at all. A word of caution regarding the blackout: it is somewhat absurd to use a blackout as a transition, if the audience can still see shadowy figures of the actors or dancers scurry into place. Unless you have a genuine blackout that renders the players completely invisible, it is more powerful to see the player move consciously into whatever will happen next, once again privileging the performance and the performer over the technical considerations.

As you stage your **performance plan**, think about moving from the **palette of stillness**. Balance choreographic motifs, vocabularies, and sweeps of large locomotor movement with groupings and stage pictures that emphasize the 'power in reserve' that stillness suggests, staying mindful of sightlines. It goes without saying that a scene staged in stillness could frustrate a portion of the audience if one player along their sightline blocks another for too long, or, in a black box, if the action is downstage on the floor so only the front few rows can see it.

Clear sightlines are an obvious element of staging and yet forgetting them still happens, particularly in the intimate theatre where there is no benefit of the distanced proscenium framing the action to sit back and observe the full stage picture. It is as much a responsibility of the player as the director or stager to make those subtle shifts (sometime even from one foot to another) that will allow the speakers to come into focus so that they are blocked for only the briefest moments. Think about Chris Cran's framing device and take note of how your work is framed. Play the role of the observer, keeping a cinematic eye on things from all points of view.

Because we are fortunate enough to build most of our shows in the Big Secret Theatre, the spacing of our staging has largely happened in rehearsal, but if that is not the case in your process, the first time you hit the deck, finesse things, expanding or contracting your blocking to best fill the space. Jamming the action downstage in a claustrophobic cluster or forcing it too far upstage because that is where you did it in rehearsal is easily fixed in a spacing rehearsal so that the lights can be focused efficiently and your staging will look its best. It all comes down to your aesthetic choice, but just be conscious that a staging concept you find thrilling, works for the audience too.

When all is done, the show is lit and cued, the actors are in full stride, it's time for the director to play. Like any long time collaborators, the OYR ensemble has a bunch of almost joking terms, which actually have fast and immediate application. Blake 'puts a knob on everything', an amusing direction that means he can turn any element onstage up or down and the ensemble is quick to 'bigger it up' or 'smaller it down.' He believes that one of the director's most important jobs is to "advocate for the first-time viewer." He uses the knob much as a music producer might to insure that the viewer will hear, see, and comprehend the show without compromising the creative aesthetics at play. This avoids distracting the viewer or taking them out of the action because of something as simple as being unable to hear or see something.

Once again **dynamic range** is the key: if the quietest moments render a speech unheard in the house, or the loudest music threatens to deafen the audience, if the emotions fall into the overwrought place, if the focus is unclear within a monologue, or if it's too light or too dark for too long – every element can be adjusted by the director with a turn of the knob to gain the best effect. Now, of course, for an actor, a technical note that one is too quiet, too loud or can't be seen is easier to take than a note to shift the build in a monologue that has been carefully crafted. Yes, there have most definitely been moments in my career where my 'immaculately made performance' is turned up or down too late in the game and the note is not welcome! Such is the stuff of the director-actor relationship but for the most part, the respect shared throughout the working life of OYR means that we agree to use the shorthand available to us and get on with the most important work at hand, which is to present a piece of theatre to the public.

CONCLUSION

What drives us to work so tirelessly and passionately as theatre artists remains as mysterious and unanswerable a thing as climbing a mountain. It is difficult and sometimes lonely. It takes courage and it's risky. Few of us will become wealthy or famous, and we must summon great reserves of inner strength if we are to make it to the top, however we define the top. So why do we strive to achieve our place in this elusive and ephemeral art form?

Chris Cran offers a clue in talking about his relationship to his art: "Painting is more than a profession or a way of life – it's a hobby." It is a charming and wonderfully animating glimpse of what sustains him through the thrills and spills of life as a painter. A hobby is something we do for the sheer pleasure of it. We devote ourselves to it so that our lives are balanced with something that owes us nothing but enjoyment and interest. Chris's quip suggests that whether or not his work provides him with remuneration, he is fascinated and drawn to the activity because he loves visual art. He is 'fan' as much as practitioner and although he has always made his living as a painter, the form itself also rewards his attention.

And, by the way, there is no shame to letting go of a professional aspiration if that passion never becomes a paying job as well. The passion can continue as a community member to illuminate your life with joy and meaning. The community of hobby artists is a big part of any society, also contributing to the appreciative and flourishing cultural life of any city or town.

The Art of Theatre has its challenges and can be heartbreaking. If we are to make it our profession and way of life, we must love it and see it as a privilege, a devotional calling worthy of the odd sacrifice and some struggle. Nobody's life is easy, we are far too fragile and easily hurt and there are always obstacles in our path that no level of success in any field will fix. But, 'a life in the theatah' is as fantastic a vocation as any.

My sincere goal of this book has been to outline the tools for making, the solutions for breaking, and the survival systems that have worked for us at One Yellow Rabbit through good times and bad. Developing a sustainable practice that is healthful and life affirming, finding comradeship, and joining hands to build a body of work that could hold up to scrutiny and time has been a profoundly challenging and rewarding journey.

As I begin my sixties, I am deeply grateful that I can look back on my life's work with pride and joy and that my memories are full of rich emotions. In no way am I done yet, but there is some kind of reckoning when asked to record one's experience and gleanings, that feels like a summing up of all the parts and inevitably leads to the question of was it all worth it? My answer is an unqualified yes. Yes. Yes! I have lived my creativity, I have used my body and the abilities I was privileged with, to their full potential. I have battled fear and sorrow and developed strength and hope. Curiosity has stretched my intellect and introduced me to remarkable ideas, discoveries, and people.

As a young dancer moving around the country, I suffered the loneliness of the young artist adrift in the ocean

The Lab: A final gathering with the Labbits after performances. Many Lab pieces have gone on to pubic performance.

of possibilities and dreamed about a community of like-minded others to work and play with. In receiving perhaps the greatest gift of all, I found that community, that posse, those friends and colleagues who helped me and taught me, and loved me. It hasn't been easy, it continues to be hard, but this was the life I wanted and this is the life I got. I wish every reader the same. If this missive has any value it will be that in your hands these tools will also be active and useful. That you forge your own body of work and that your life is the one you want and the one you get.

The End

Acknowledgments

My list of acknowledgments would be lengthy and I would hate to find upon cracking the first edition that I had omitted anyone and so instead please refer to the index and with every person's name you read, know that I am deeply indebted to them all for the wisdom, knowledge, challenges, inspiration and delight their names represent. Thanks to Durvile Publications (UpRoute Books) and Lorene Shyba who supported *The Big Secret Book* every step of the way. Love and gratitude to every Labbit who has ever graced The Big Secret with their art and commitment. Thanks to the OYR Board of Directors who have stood by us through it all and to all the volunteers who give so kindly of themselves to keep our enterprise flourishing. Thanks also to Ryan Bartlett for his photo wrangling and constant graceful manner. Special thanks to Johnny Dunn, the prime minister of vibe who has been there in every way with kisses and kindness. Thanks to John and Betty Clarke for life and love. Eternal gratitude to my greatest life allies, Shawna Helland and Anne Georg in whose eyes I look to stay the course. And especially to Chris Cran, the best of the best and my heart's content.

Index

Aitken, Will 65
Alexander, Frederick Matthias 28
Alexander Technique 28
Alien Bait 100
All The Little Animals I've Eaten 97
America 118
Antigone Undone 64–65
Art of Literature, The 148
Banff Centre 107
Barrett, Andrew 67
Bartenieff Fundamentals 27
Bartenieff, Irmgard 27
Barthes, Roland 93–96
Bartlett, Ryan iv, 190
Bazin, André 64
Beautiful Losers 16
Beckett, Samuel 86
Bellamy, Mark 85
Bidini, Dave 168
Big Secret Theatre 6, 107, 112, 186
Binoche, Juliet 64–65
Blake, William 137
Bowie, David 110
Brecht, Bertold 86

Breeder 84–85
Brooker, Blake 6–198
Burns, Grant 82
Burns, Lindsay 85
Burroughs, William S. 109–119, 117
Cabaret 60–61
Cadger, Neil 27, 90
Camera Lucida: Reflections on Photography 93
Campbell, Joseph 90–91
Carson, Anne 65
Carson McCullers 134–136
Changing Bodies 97
Chapel of Extreme Experience 118
Charlton, Jeff 25
Chaton, A.E. 98
Cheesman, Keshia 25
Christian, Scott 118
Christmann, Mark 90
Cohen, Leonard 16–17, 55, 66, 133
Communion: A True Story 100
Cooper, David 9
Coward, Noël 72
Cran, Chris 7–198
Curtis, Andy 6–198
Damien Frost 103
Dawkins, Alexandra 185
Death in New Orleans 103
Deleeuw, Johanne 133, 135
Demeanor, Kris i, 112
Dennie, Sean 21, 76
de Wilde, Brandon 135
Doing Leonard Cohen 16–18

Dreamachine Plans 118
Dream Machine, The 117–121
Duthie, Christopher 134
Elevator Repair Service Theatre 150
Elton, Heather i, 4, 51
Erotic Irony of Old Glory 90
Fabulous Disaster 76, 97
Fat Jack Falstaff's Last Hour 36–37, 103
Featherland 85, 97
Feldenkrais Method 28
Feldenkrais, Moshé 28
Fitzgerald, F. Scott 150
Five Hole, Tales of Hockey Erotica 168
Flynn, Anne i, 50–51
Fortean Times 100
Geiger, John 118
Gershwin, George 77
Gilbertson, Onalea 118, 168
Ginsberg, Allen 118
Great Gatsby, The 150
Green, Michael 6–198
Grotowski, Jerzy 86
Gutiérrez, Zaide Silvia i
Gysin, Brion 110, 117–118
Hackney, Peggy 44
Hall, Matthew 25–198
Hara, Manami 182
Harris, Julie 135
Her Kind 170
High Performance Rodeo 75, 103
Hines, Karen i, 97, 112
Hinton, Peter ii, 59, 112

History of Wild Theatre, The 101
Hoffman, Albert 117
How To Speak Poetry 66
Hughes, Ted 168
Hunt, Chris 112
Huxley, Aldous 117
Inkster, Alexandria 159
Joyce, James 104, 106
Kawasaki Exit 135, 180–182
Kennedy, Fiona 134
Kids In the Hall 130
Koranyi, Jakob ii, 112
Laban Movement Analysis 27–31, 43–49
Laban, Rudolf 27–31
Labbits 25–198
Lamb, Warren 48
Land the Animals, The 97
Laws, The 160–162
Lorrain, Claude 86
Lowell, Robert 168
MacEachern, Patrick 182
Martini, Clem ii
McCulloch, Bruce 112, 130
McDowell, Richard 6, 121, 134–135
McKinney, Matt 27–198
Member of the Wedding, The 134
Miranda, Bianca 25
Miserere 145
Moller, Peter 118
Monk, Davida 112
Morrow, Martin ii
Munich Now 182

Murrell, John ii, 1–3, 7, 36, 103–107, 176
National Gallery of Canada 83, 97
Nijinsky, Vaslav 175
One Yellow Rabbit 1–198
Pain Killer 119–121
Pallagi, Elise 25
Pärt, Arvo 145
Payne, Brad 118
Permission 84
Plath, Sylvia 133, 168–170, 181
Plato 160–162
Portrait of the Artist as a Young Man, A 104
Poussin, Nicholas 86
Radiohead 151
Radioheaded 2 112
Rheostatics, The 168
Rhymer, David ii, 34, 117
Rilke, Rainer Maria 11, 171
Rite of Spring, The 175
Schechner, Richard 115
Schopenhauer, Arthur 148
Schroeder, Stephen 82
Sexton, Anne 133, 168, 181
Sign Language 21
Simamba, Makambe K. 55
Smash Cut Freeze 134–136
Smith, Patti 110
Sniatyski, Caroline 139
Somalia Yellow 101
Sommerville, Ian 117

Stanislavski Method 37
Stepkowski, Elizabeth 35
Stickland, Eugene ii
Stravinsky, Igor 175
Strieber, Whitley 100
Swir, Anna 145
Sylvia Plath Must Not Die 168–170, 181
Taking Shakespeare 103
Tan, Mike 36, 59
Tears Of A Dinosaur 39
Tekakwitha, Catherine 16
Theagenes the Boxer 160–162
Tigress At The City Gates 34–35
Torre, William 114
Tzeng, Pamela 161
van Belle, David 115, 118
Van Hove, Ivo 65
WAG! 75–77
Ware, Heather 95
Wasteland, The 59
Waters, Ethel 135
What The Thunder Said 59, 135
Whitacre, Eric 77
Wild Theatre: The History of One Yellow Rabbit ii
Wiseman, Bobby 112
Wustenberg, Russell 163
Yorke, Thom 110
Zelle, Margaretha 34
Zweigard, Lulu 28

About the Author

Denise Clarke is the Associate Artist of One Yellow Rabbit Theatre and a permanent member of the OYR Creation Ensemble. Clarke stages and performs original work for the stage and has established a national and international touring profile, as well as choreographing, acting, and directing with various companies across Canada. She was made a Fellow of the Royal Canadian Geographical Society, received an Honourary Doctorate from the University of Calgary, and is a Member of the Order of Canada.